Part I: The Making of an Emperor

1. Genghis Kh A Prince's Up

Early life and education with the Mongol court

Kublai Khan's formative years, spent within the dynamic and often brutal crucible of the Mongol court, profoundly shaped his worldview and leadership style. Unlike many Western rulers who received a formalized education in classical subjects, Kublai's learning was a far more practical and experiential affair, steeped in the realities of nomadic life and the intricacies of Mongol power politics.

Born in 1215, Kublai was the fourth son of Tolui, Genghis Khan's youngest son, and Sorghaghtani Beki, a woman of remarkable intelligence and political acumen. This lineage alone placed him at the heart of Mongol imperial power, ensuring a privileged upbringing unlike that of most. His **early education** wasn't confined to the formal classroom; rather, it was a multifaceted immersion in the military and political landscapes of the expanding Mongol Empire. He witnessed firsthand the strategies and tactics of his grandfather, Genghis Khan, learning the art of war not from books but from **observing firsthand the conquest and consolidation of vast territories**.

The <u>Mongol court</u> itself was a demanding classroom. It was a place of constant maneuvering, where alliances shifted like desert sands, and survival often depended on astute political judgment. Kublai learned to navigate this complex web of family relationships, competing factions, and ambitious individuals. He observed the ways in which his grandfather and uncles wielded power, studying their successes and failures, internalizing the lessons of both masterful strategy and devastating error. This **practical political education** proved invaluable in his later life, allowing him to deftly manage the diverse and often conflicting interests within his own empire.

His upbringing also instilled in him a deep understanding of Mongol culture and traditions. He learned horsemanship, archery, and the essential skills of a nomadic warrior. This wasn't merely physical training; it was about mastering the ways of the steppe, gaining the respect and loyalty of his fellow Mongols, and understanding their culture's values and priorities. This <u>cultural grounding</u> served as a cornerstone of his rule, enabling him to effectively govern a diverse population ranging from seasoned Mongols to the sophisticated Chinese.

Beyond military prowess and political acumen, Kublai's education embraced a broader intellectual curiosity. While the Mongol court didn't possess the scholastic environment of a European court, it actively engaged with various cultures and religions. Kublai was exposed to *Buddhist philosophy*, gaining an appreciation for its spiritual depth. He also encountered different forms of governance and administration, absorbing lessons from both the conquered and allied populations. This **eclectic learning process**, though informal, provided a solid foundation for his future endeavors as a ruler.

Table of Contents

In summary, Kublai Khan's early life and education wasn't a traditional one. Instead of formal schools, he had the bustling Mongol court, the vast plains of the empire, and the battlefield as his classrooms. His education was a practical, experiential immersion in the complexities of leadership, politics, warfare, and diverse cultures. This unique upbringing shaped his exceptional leadership abilities, his ambition, and his vision for a vast and integrated empire, enabling him to ultimately bridge empires and leave an indelible mark on world history.

- A Glimpse into the Crucible of Power -

Military Training and Strategic Insights from His Grandfather

The formative years of Kublai Khan, grandson of the legendary Genghis Khan, were profoundly shaped by the military prowess and strategic acumen of his grandfather. This wasn't merely a matter of familial influence; it represented a direct and intentional grooming for leadership within the burgeoning Mongol Empire.

While historical accounts vary in detail, a consistent theme emerges: Kublai's education wasn't confined to the traditional scholarly pursuits of the era. Instead, his training emphasized **practical military skills and strategic thinking**. Genghis Khan, a master strategist himself, recognized the potential in his grandson and personally oversaw aspects of his military education. This involved more than simply observing campaigns; it constituted active participation in the very fabric of Mongol military life.

Kublai was likely exposed to **rigorous physical training** from a young age, learning horsemanship, archery, and other essential skills of Mongol warriors. These weren't just exercises; they were integral to the development of discipline, stamina, and the ability to operate effectively under pressure – all crucial components for a future military leader. Beyond physical prowess, the emphasis on **tactical awareness** was equally paramount.

Genghis Khan's legacy extends beyond his conquests; it lies in the innovative military strategies he devised and implemented. Kublai, as a keen observer, would have been privy to the inner workings of these strategies. He would have witnessed firsthand **Genghis Khan's masterful use of mobility, his ability to exploit weaknesses in enemy formations, and his shrewd understanding of terrain and logistics**. These weren't abstract concepts; they were lessons learned through direct observation and likely through participation in smaller-scale engagements under the watchful eye of experienced commanders.

Moreover, the accounts suggest **a mentorship beyond simple military drills**. Genghis Khan likely imparted his strategic philosophy, emphasizing the importance of calculated risk, adaptability in the face of unforeseen circumstances, and the crucial role of intelligence gathering. The emphasis on swift and decisive action, coupled with a deep understanding of the enemy's strengths and weaknesses, would have been central to this mentorship. Kublai may have also been exposed to the intricacies of Mongol diplomacy and the crucial role it played in expanding and securing the Empire's borders. The art of negotiation, alliance-building, and understanding diverse cultures were skills critical for a future leader of such a vast and diverse realm.

The interaction between grandson and grandfather wasn't solely transactional. The relationship, though rooted in hierarchical structure, likely involved a degree of **mutual respect and shared ambition**. Genghis Khan saw in Kublai a promising successor, while Kublai likely recognized the value of learning from one of history's most successful military commanders. This intergenerational exchange of knowledge profoundly influenced Kublai's subsequent military campaigns and his leadership of the Mongol Empire, ultimately shaping the course of history.

In conclusion, Kublai Khan's military training extended beyond mere physical conditioning. It encompassed a profound immersion in the strategic thinking and tactical brilliance that defined Genghis Khan's legacy. This immersive education, a combination of practical experience and philosophical guidance, laid the groundwork for Kublai's own impressive military accomplishments and his ultimate success in solidifying and expanding the Mongol Empire.

Witnessing the Expansion of the Mongol Empire Firsthand

Kublai Khan's formative years were inextricably linked to the relentless expansion of the Mongol Empire, an experience that profoundly shaped his worldview and leadership style. Unlike many rulers who inherited a stable realm, Kublai witnessed firsthand the breathtaking scale and brutal efficiency of his grandfather, Genghis Khan's, conquests. This firsthand exposure wasn't merely a passive observation; it was a deeply immersive education in imperial power, military strategy, and the complexities of managing a vast and diverse empire.

From a young age, Kublai was privy to the strategic planning, the logistical marvels, and the sheer brutality of Mongol military campaigns. He wouldn't have just *heard* tales of sieges and conquests; he would have *seen* the meticulously organized armies, the innovative tactics employed, and the swift, decisive victories that redefined the geopolitical landscape of Eurasia. He witnessed the subjugation of powerful kingdoms, the incorporation of diverse peoples into the Mongol fold, and the establishment of trade routes that connected distant civilizations. This was not a theoretical understanding of empire; it was a visceral, lived experience.

The scale of the Mongol Empire's expansion during Kublai's youth must be emphasized. We're not talking about incremental territorial gains; the empire was expanding at a truly unprecedented pace. Vast swathes of land, from the steppes of Central Asia to the fertile plains of China, were being brought under Mongol control, often with astonishing speed. Kublai would have witnessed the collapse of established dynasties, the displacement of populations, and the chaotic yet ultimately effective process of incorporating conquered territories into the empire's structure.

The **impact** of this constant expansion on the young Kublai was multifaceted. He saw firsthand the power of unified command, the effectiveness of carefully planned campaigns, and the necessity of swift, decisive action. He also saw the human cost of such rapid expansion—the bloodshed, the displacement, and the resistance that often flared up in conquered regions. This understanding of both the triumphs and tragedies of conquest would significantly influence his own future strategies and policies as emperor. It would inform his approach to governance, his treatment of conquered populations, and his understanding of the challenges of maintaining such a vast and diverse empire.

The Mongol military campaigns were not just about brute force; they were sophisticated undertakings involving careful logistics, intricate diplomacy, and a willingness to adapt to diverse circumstances. Kublai would have seen this firsthand, observing how the Mongols skillfully navigated complex political landscapes, formed strategic alliances, and employed a combination of military force and shrewd negotiations to achieve their goals. This practical education in statecraft would prove invaluable as he ascended to power.

Furthermore, the expansion of the Mongol Empire wasn't simply a military undertaking; it was a catalyst for significant **cultural exchange**. The merging of diverse societies under Mongol rule, though often violent in its initial stages, resulted in the transmission of ideas, technologies, and cultural practices. Kublai would have witnessed this firsthand, observing the interaction of different ethnic groups within the empire's framework. This exposure to diverse cultures and perspectives undoubtedly broadened his understanding of the world and informed his policies concerning religious tolerance and intercultural relations.

In essence, Kublai Khan's witnessing of the Mongol Empire's expansion wasn't merely a historical event; it was a formative experience that shaped his character, his worldview, and ultimately, his reign as emperor. It wasn't simply about observing the growth of an empire; it was about learning the complex interplay of military prowess, political acumen, cultural adaptation, and the profound impact of power on individuals and societies.

Conclusion:

The expansion of the Mongol Empire during Kublai Khan's formative years provided him with a unique and profound education in the arts of war, diplomacy, and governance. This firsthand exposure directly influenced his leadership style, his approach to governing a vast and diverse empire, and his approach to both internal and external relations. This early life experience is fundamental to understanding the complexities of his reign and his lasting legacy.

His relationship with his father and brothers

A complex tapestry woven with threads of ambition, loyalty, and rivalry, Kublai Khan's relationships with his father, Tolui, and his brothers formed a crucial backdrop to his rise to power and shaped the trajectory of his reign. Understanding these dynamics is key to comprehending the man behind the emperor.

Tolui, Kublai's father, was the youngest son of Genghis Khan, yet his influence within the family and the empire was immense. Unlike some of his elder brothers who wielded power through military might, Tolui possessed a shrewd political acumen and a calmer, more strategic approach. His relationship with Kublai was not one of outright dominance, but rather of mentorship and subtle guidance. Tolui instilled in Kublai a strong sense of political strategy, a keen understanding of diplomacy, and an appreciation for the importance of securing alliances. While military prowess was valued in the Mongol culture, Tolui seemingly cultivated in Kublai a more nuanced appreciation for political maneuvering, a skill that proved invaluable in Kublai's later ascension and governance of the Yuan Dynasty.

The relationship between Kublai and his brothers, however, was markedly different. Marked by intense competition for power and succession within the Mongol lineage, their interactions were often fraught with tension and underlying rivalry. While sources detailing specific events between Kublai and his brothers are sometimes scarce or contradictory, the historical record consistently suggests a climate of constant maneuvering, strategic alliances, and occasional open conflict. This competitive atmosphere significantly shaped Kublai's character and his strategies to consolidate power. The desire to surpass his brothers, to prove his worthiness to the Mongol legacy, pushed him to achieve remarkable feats of leadership and military success.

While specific incidents are difficult to definitively detail, it's evident that Kublai's brothers posed a constant threat to his ambitions. The struggle for the succession to the Great Khanate after the deaths of Ögedei and Güyük was particularly turbulent. Kublai's maneuvering during this period showcases both his diplomatic finesse and his unwavering determination to secure the ultimate prize. The alliances he formed, the rivals he neutralized – these actions all stemmed from a deep understanding of the familial power struggles that characterized the Mongol world. His success in overcoming his brothers' challenges not only elevated him to the throne but also profoundly shaped his approach to governing his vast empire.

The legacy of these familial relationships is significant. While his father's influence was subtle yet profound, shaping Kublai's strategic mindset, the rivalry with his brothers hardened his resolve and honed his political skills.

This complex interplay of familial ties, competition, and mentorship created a multifaceted leader, one whose reign was marked by both ambition and a profound understanding of the delicate balance required to govern a multi-ethnic empire spanning continents. His success, therefore, cannot be separated from the crucible of his relationships with his father and his brothers – a dynamic that casts a long shadow over his historical legacy.

Kublai Khan's journey to power wasn't a solo expedition. It was a carefully orchestrated dance amongst familial bonds and bitter rivalries. These relationships ultimately shaped his leadership style, his approach to governance, and the enduring impact of the Yuan Dynasty on world history. To truly grasp the magnitude of Kublai Khan's achievements, one must delve into the intricacies of these complex and often turbulent familial dynamics.

2. The Rise of a Leader: Consolidation of Power

Early Military Campaigns and Strategic Victories

Kublai Khan's ascent to power was not solely a matter of inheritance; it was forged in the crucible of relentless military campaigns and punctuated by strategically brilliant victories that solidified his claim to the Mongol throne and laid the foundation for the Yuan Dynasty.

Before inheriting the vast Mongol Empire, Kublai Khan honed his military skills and strategic acumen through a series of decisive engagements. These campaigns were not mere power grabs; they were carefully orchestrated moves aimed at consolidating his position within the complex web of Mongol power politics and expanding the empire's influence.

One of his earliest significant campaigns targeted the **Tangut kingdom of Xi Xia**. This campaign, launched in the **1220s**, demonstrated Kublai Khan's early mastery of siege warfare and his ability to effectively manage logistics across challenging terrains. The Tangut, despite their initial resistance, eventually succumbed to the relentless pressure of the Mongol forces, highlighting Kublai's tactical prowess in adapting to diverse challenges presented by different enemies.

The conquest of Xi Xia wasn't simply a military victory; it was a strategic masterstroke. The territory's annexation provided Kublai Khan with valuable resources, including manpower and strategic positioning to launch further expeditions southward toward the **Southern Song Dynasty**. His success here proved his competence as a military commander and further strengthened his legitimacy among Mongol nobles.

The subsequent **campaigns against the Southern Song Dynasty** were even more ambitious and demanding. They showcased not only his military capabilities but also his strategic planning and understanding of long-term goals. Unlike many brutal Mongol conquests, Kublai Khan's approach involved a complex interplay of military force and diplomatic maneuvering. He meticulously studied the Southern Song's strengths and weaknesses, adapting his strategies to exploit their vulnerabilities.

One example of Kublai's strategic brilliance lies in his understanding of **naval warfare**. Recognizing the importance of controlling the seas, he invested heavily in developing a powerful Mongol navy. This allowed his forces to launch successful attacks on coastal cities and effectively cut off Southern Song supply lines. The naval victories were crucial, demonstrating his willingness to adapt his military capabilities to encompass areas that were previously neglected under Mongol leadership.

Kublai Khan's approach also involved incorporating advanced siege tactics and innovative weaponry. He employed **Mongol catapults** and other siege engines effectively against fortified cities. While his military prowess was undeniable, he was also a pragmatic leader, understanding that lengthy sieges could be costly. He frequently used a combination of military threats and diplomatic overtures to influence city leaders to surrender, minimizing unnecessary bloodshed and maximizing efficiency.

The **fall of Xiangyang in 1273**, a strategically important city with formidable defenses, marked a turning point in the conquest of the Southern Song. The protracted siege, which tested Kublai Khan's patience and logistical abilities, showcased his persistence and determination. The subsequent capture of **Lin'an (modern-day Hangzhou), the Southern Song capital, in 1276**, was the culmination of years of careful planning and relentless military campaigns. This victory signified the complete subjugation of the Southern Song and the establishment of Kublai Khan's dominance over all of China.

In summary, Kublai Khan's early military campaigns were not mere acts of aggression, but carefully planned operations showcasing his strategic brilliance and adaptation. His tactical mastery, coupled with skillful diplomacy, resourcefulness, and a persistent drive for success, allowed him to achieve decisive victories that proved instrumental in his rise to power and the establishment of the Yuan Dynasty.

Navigating Family Politics and Rivalries within the Mongol Elite

Kublai Khan's ascent to power was far from a straightforward succession. The Mongol world, even at the height of its imperial glory, was a complex web of familial alliances, bitter rivalries, and ruthless power struggles. Understanding Kublai's navigation of this treacherous political landscape is crucial to grasping his eventual triumph and the establishment of the Yuan Dynasty.

The death of Genghis Khan in 1227 did not bring about a peaceful transition. His vast empire was divided amongst his sons, sparking immediate tensions and competition for dominance. While Ögedei Khan, Genghis's chosen successor, reigned, the seeds of future conflict were sown. Kublai, as a grandson of Genghis, found himself within a family dynamic rife with ambition, jealousy, and shifting loyalties. His uncles, brothers, and even cousins represented potential threats to his own aspirations.

The struggle for influence within the Mongol court was often brutal and unforgiving. Alliances were forged and broken with alarming frequency, as individuals jockeyed for position and access to power. Kublai had to expertly navigate these intricate relationships, carefully cultivating alliances while neutralizing rivals. This required a deft touch, a deep understanding of Mongol culture, and a willingness to employ both diplomacy and, when necessary, force.

One of the key challenges Kublai faced was the rivalry between different branches of the Genghisid family. The different lineages held differing levels of influence and power, creating an environment of intense competition. Kublai had to demonstrate his own strength and legitimacy while simultaneously appeasing or outmaneuvering more established branches of the family. This involved strategic marriages, careful selection of advisors, and a constant assessment of the shifting balance of power.

Beyond the purely familial conflicts, Kublai also had to contend with broader political factions within the Mongol elite. Different tribal groups and powerful nobles held sway, often pursuing their own agendas. Kublai's ability to garner support from influential figures across these diverse groups was a testament to his political acumen. He skillfully balanced the needs and ambitions of various factions, forging temporary alliances and utilizing patronage to secure their loyalty.

His relationship with his brother Ariq Böke is a particularly compelling case study. Their rivalry escalated into open warfare, a civil war that threatened to tear apart the Mongol Empire. Kublai's eventual victory, despite the fierce opposition, highlights his strategic prowess and resolute determination. This conflict not only demonstrated Kublai's strength but also served to consolidate his position as the undisputed leader.

Kublai's success in managing these complex political dynamics was not solely a matter of strength or ruthlessness. He demonstrated a remarkable ability to understand and utilize the intricacies of Mongol kinship and tribal structure. He skillfully played on existing loyalties and divisions, manipulating alliances to achieve his goals. His understanding of the nuances of Mongol political culture, combined with his shrewd political judgment, allowed him to rise above his rivals and establish himself as the paramount leader.

In conclusion, the journey to becoming the Great Khan was a testament to Kublai Khan's political acumen and his mastery of intricate family politics. His ability to navigate the treacherous waters of Mongol elite rivalries, skillfully forming alliances and neutralizing opponents, ultimately paved the way for the founding of the Yuan Dynasty and his position as one of history's most significant figures.

Development of Diplomatic Skills and Alliances

Kublai Khan's ascent to power was not solely predicated on military prowess; it was significantly shaped by his astute cultivation of diplomatic relationships and strategic alliances. This skill, honed from a young age amidst the complex political landscape of the Mongol court, proved crucial in consolidating his authority and expanding his empire.

While inheriting a legacy of conquest from his grandfather, Genghis Khan, Kublai understood the limitations of purely military dominance. **Maintaining a vast, multicultural empire** required more than brute force; it demanded a delicate balance of power, shrewd negotiation, and the ability to forge lasting alliances.

One of Kublai's earliest demonstrations of diplomatic acumen was his approach to **managing internal Mongol factions**. The Mongol aristocracy, though unified under Genghis Khan, was composed of numerous clans and lineages, each vying for influence and power. Kublai skillfully navigated these complex family dynamics, utilizing both kinship ties and calculated concessions to secure the loyalty of key figures. This intricate web of alliances proved vital in preventing internal strife and consolidating his claim to the throne.

Beyond the internal realm, Kublai recognized the importance of forging **alliances with external powers**. The conquered territories of China, with their long history of sophisticated diplomacy, presented a significant challenge. Unlike his predecessors who often relied on subjugation, Kublai adopted a more nuanced approach, incorporating elements of Chinese statecraft into his own governance.

He understood the necessity of gaining the **support of the Chinese elite**, many of whom initially resisted Mongol rule. Kublai implemented policies aimed at appeasing the Confucian scholar-officials, recognizing their crucial role in administration and social order. He promoted qualified Chinese individuals to high positions within his government, thereby integrating them into the ruling structure and fostering a sense of shared governance. This was a sharp departure from the purely military-driven policies of earlier Mongol leaders and exemplified his evolving diplomatic strategy.

Furthermore, Kublai engaged in **extensive diplomatic exchanges with foreign powers**. He sent and received embassies to and from distant kingdoms, fostering trade relationships and securing alliances. These interactions went beyond simple transactional agreements; they involved the exchange of cultural artifacts, scholarly texts, and religious emissaries, fostering understanding and establishing networks of mutual benefit. This approach underscored his vision of a globally interconnected empire, a testament to his advanced diplomatic thinking.

The **success of his diplomatic endeavors** is reflected in the relative stability and prosperity of the Yuan Dynasty during the initial decades of his reign. While challenges and rebellions certainly arose, Kublai's skillful use of diplomacy allowed him to effectively address many of them before they escalated into major conflicts, illustrating the effectiveness of his strategy.

In conclusion, Kublai Khan's diplomatic skills played an integral role in the formation and stability of the Yuan Dynasty. His mastery of internal politics, his strategic integration of Chinese elites, and his active pursuit of foreign alliances demonstrate his unique understanding of imperial leadership. He transcended the purely military approach of his predecessors, proving that diplomacy, when carefully cultivated, could be as powerful, if not more so, than conquest itself. His legacy serves as a testament to the enduring significance of strategic diplomacy in building and maintaining a vast and lasting empire.

The Establishment of His Authority and Influence

Kublai Khan's ascension to supreme power within the Mongol Empire was a complex process, marked by both strategic brilliance and ruthless pragmatism. This section will delve into the multifaceted strategies he employed to solidify his rule, moving beyond simple conquest to encompass the subtle art of governance and the cultivation of loyalty.

Initially, Kublai faced significant challenges. While inheriting a vast empire from his ancestors, the legacy of Genghis Khan also cast a long shadow. He had to navigate intricate family politics, contending with ambitious relatives and powerful factions vying for control. The death of his brother, **Möngke Khan**, triggered a power struggle, with Kublai's rivals, such as **Ariq Böke**, actively challenging his claim to the throne. Kublai's response was swift and decisive. He skillfully leveraged his military prowess and political acumen to defeat Ariq Böke in a brutal civil war. This victory, while bloody, was essential in establishing his dominance and consolidating power. It sent a clear message: disobedience would be met with swift and merciless retribution.

Beyond military might, Kublai demonstrated a keen understanding of the importance of **legitimacy**. He strategically courted the support of influential figures within Mongol society, forging alliances with key clans and families. He generously rewarded loyalty, while harshly punishing treachery. This shrewd approach, blending carrots and sticks, proved instrumental in gradually solidifying his rule and garnering the support of many who previously remained ambivalent or openly hostile. His adoption of a more sophisticated court system, incorporating elements from conquered territories and demonstrating his understanding of the intricacies of governing a diverse empire, also significantly added to the strength of his position.

His interactions with the **Chinese population** also played a crucial role in cementing his authority. While initially wary of Mongol rule, Kublai implemented policies designed to win over the hearts and minds of his subjects. He demonstrated a pragmatic approach to governance, adapting Mongol traditions to existing Chinese administrative structures and gradually integrating the two systems. This calculated blend of cultural sensitivity and firm control demonstrated his mastery of statecraft and facilitated a smoother transition of power.

Kublai's **religious tolerance** further bolstered his authority. He recognized the diverse religious landscape of his empire, and rather than impose a single faith, he showed respect for Buddhism, Taoism, Confucianism, Islam, and Christianity. This fostered an atmosphere of relative harmony, reducing the likelihood of rebellion fueled by religious tensions. His patronage of the arts and the fostering of cultural exchange across his vast empire enhanced his image as a benevolent and enlightened ruler, fostering loyalty and cementing his position as the legitimate emperor.

Furthermore, Kublai's emphasis on **economic development** further strengthened his reign. By investing in infrastructure projects, promoting trade along the Silk Road, and implementing sensible economic policies, he generated prosperity within his realm. A prosperous populace was less likely to rebel, creating a more stable foundation for his rule. The economic growth under his reign contributed to his image as a successful and capable leader, reinforcing his position of authority.

In conclusion, Kublai Khan's establishment of authority and influence was not a singular event but a carefully orchestrated campaign involving military dominance, astute political maneuvering, cultural diplomacy, economic prosperity, and the cultivation of loyalty across diverse populations. It was a testament to his exceptional leadership abilities and his deep understanding of the complexities of managing a vast and multi-ethnic empire. His reign exemplified the delicate balance between brute force and shrewd governance essential for establishing and maintaining control over such an extensive realm, creating a lasting impact on the history of the Mongol empire and the world.

3. Conquests and Consolidation: Subduing the Southern Song

Military Strategies Employed Against the Southern Song Dynasty

Kublai Khan's conquest of the Southern Song Dynasty, the final phase in the Mongol unification of China, wasn't a simple blitzkrieg. It was a protracted campaign demanding innovative military strategies to overcome the Song's formidable defenses and resilience. The Song, though militarily weaker than the Mongols, possessed geographic advantages and a seasoned navy.

One key element of Kublai Khan's strategy was the **combined arms approach**. He understood the necessity of integrating diverse military units to exploit vulnerabilities. Mongol cavalry, renowned for their mobility and shock tactics, spearheaded many offensives. However, Kublai also deployed significant numbers of *Chinese infantry*, leveraging their experience in siege warfare and their familiarity with the terrain. This synergistic combination proved decisive in many battles.

The **siege warfare** employed by the Mongols underwent a significant evolution during this conflict. While the Mongols were masters of swift, decisive cavalry actions, the Song's strong coastal and city fortifications required a more patient and methodical approach. Kublai's forces adapted, mastering advanced siege techniques and employing powerful siege weaponry, including *mangonels*, *trebuchets*, and other siege engines. The prolonged sieges, while costly in resources, effectively depleted the Song's defenses and broke their will to resist.

A crucial aspect of Kublai Khan's success was his **strategic understanding of logistics and supply lines**. Maintaining a vast army across challenging terrain required meticulous planning and execution. The Mongols developed sophisticated networks for transporting supplies and reinforcements, often utilizing waterways and established trade routes. This logistical prowess enabled sustained military pressure on the Song, preventing them from effectively regrouping or receiving significant external support.

Furthermore, Kublai Khan skillfully employed **psychological warfare**. His reputation as an invincible conqueror spread fear among the Song's population, undermining their morale and resistance. Selective displays of power, coupled with offers of surrender and lenient treatment to those who submitted, helped to fracture the Song's defense and facilitate the conquest of strategic cities and regions without prolonged and costly sieges.

Naval power played a pivotal role. Although initially less adept at naval warfare, Kublai Khan invested heavily in *building a formidable Mongol navy*. This allowed the Mongols to blockade key coastal cities, disrupting supply lines and cutting off Song reinforcements, weakening their defense and bolstering Mongol victories on land. The Mongol navy proved particularly crucial in the final stages of the campaign.

Finally, the Mongols also showed their understanding of **political and economic warfare**. They targeted key economic centers and infrastructure, crippling the Song's ability to fund their resistance and maintain their war effort. This strategic approach, combined with the military pressure, created a perfect storm that ultimately led to the fall of the Southern Song Dynasty and the establishment of Yuan Dynasty. The nuanced approach, blending direct military force with strategic resource management and psychological manipulation, highlighted Kublai Khan's exceptional military acumen.

The conquest of the Southern Song wasn't merely a display of brute force; it was a testament to Kublai Khan's ability to adapt, innovate, and integrate diverse military assets to achieve his strategic objectives.

Key battles and sieges, analysis of tactics and logistics

Kublai Khan's military campaigns were instrumental in the establishment and expansion of the Yuan Dynasty. His strategies, a blend of Mongol ferocity and pragmatic adaptation to Chinese warfare, resulted in significant victories but also faced notable setbacks. A detailed examination of key battles reveals the complexities of his military approach and the logistical challenges of commanding a vast empire.

The siege of Xiangyang (1268-1273) stands as a pivotal moment, demonstrating Kublai Khan's strategic patience and technological prowess. Xiangyang, a heavily fortified city on the Yangtze River, was the key to controlling the Southern Song Dynasty's remaining territory. The Mongol forces, initially reliant on traditional siege tactics, faced prolonged resistance. Kublai Khan's innovation lay in employing sophisticated siege weaponry, including advanced catapults and possibly even early forms of gunpowder weapons, overcoming the city's formidable defenses. **The prolonged siege also highlights the logistical complexities** of supplying a massive army over several years, necessitating an intricate network of supply lines and resource management. The ultimate capture of Xiangyang not only opened the path to the Song capital but also demonstrated the effectiveness of a combined approach – brute force supplemented by technological superiority and strategic planning.

The battle of Yamen (1279), the final decisive clash against the Southern Song, showcased the Mongols' adaptability on water. While primarily a land-based power, Kublai Khan constructed a formidable navy. The battle itself demonstrated the Mongols' masterful use of combined arms tactics, integrating naval power with land-based forces. **The Song navy, despite valiant efforts, was outmatched by the sheer size and organizational capacity of the Mongol fleet.** The defeat at Yamen marked the end of the Southern Song Dynasty and solidified the Yuan Dynasty's control over all of China. The logistical undertaking of building and maintaining a powerful navy, particularly considering the Mongol's limited experience in naval warfare, underscores the ambition and foresight of Kublai Khan's campaign planning.

However, not all of Kublai Khan's military endeavors were successful. His attempts to conquer *Japan* in 1274 and 1281 resulted in devastating defeats. These campaigns exposed the limitations of even the most powerful armies when confronted with unforeseen circumstances. The **typhoons, known as "kamikaze," that decimated the Mongol fleets** highlight the role of unpredictable environmental factors in military strategy. **Logistically, the immense undertaking of transporting and supplying a vast army across the sea proved incredibly challenging.** The scale of the expedition and its ultimately failed outcome underscore the inherent risks in extending the empire's reach beyond easily defensible boundaries. These campaigns served as a stark reminder that even the most carefully planned and well-executed military strategies are not immune to the unexpected.

The **conquests in Southeast Asia**, while not as strategically significant as the Chinese campaigns, also present valuable insights into Kublai Khan's military tactics and logistics. These campaigns, often involving smaller-scale operations against diverse opponents, required adaptability and efficient resource allocation. The successes and failures of these campaigns offer valuable insights into how Kublai Khan adapted his military approach to the specific conditions of different terrains and cultures, showing the diversity in his approach to warfare.

In conclusion, an analysis of Kublai Khan's key battles and sieges reveals a complex interplay of strategic brilliance, logistical mastery, and unforeseen challenges. While his innovative tactics and unwavering determination led to significant territorial expansion and the consolidation of the Yuan Dynasty, his failures highlight the inherent limitations of even the mightiest empires and underscore the importance of anticipating unpredictable variables.

Integration of conquered territories and populations

Kublai Khan's conquest of the Southern Song Dynasty in 1279 marked a pivotal moment not only in the expansion of the Mongol Empire but also in the complex process of integrating conquered territories and diverse populations.

Unlike some of his predecessors, who often relied on brutal subjugation and mass slaughter, Kublai Khan adopted a more nuanced approach. While **military might** was certainly a key component of his strategy, he also understood the importance of *political pragmatism* and cultural adaptation in consolidating his newly acquired lands. This involved a carefully crafted blend of **coercion and cooperation**, seeking to exploit existing power structures while simultaneously introducing new administrative and economic systems.

The **integration** process was far from seamless. The Southern Song, while weakened, possessed a sophisticated bureaucratic system and a strong cultural identity that posed significant challenges to Mongol rule. **Resistance** continued in various forms long after the formal surrender of the dynasty, often fueled by resentment towards the foreign conquerors and fears of cultural erasure. This resistance manifested in rebellions, both large and small, scattered across the conquered territories. Kublai Khan responded to this with a mixture of **military suppression** and attempts at *reconciliation.*

One of the key aspects of Kublai Khan's strategy was the **selective incorporation** of Chinese elites into the administrative structure of the newly established Yuan Dynasty. Many former Song officials and scholars were appointed to positions of authority, though always under the ultimate supervision of Mongol officials. This approach served a dual purpose: it allowed the Mongols to leverage the expertise and experience of the conquered population while simultaneously defusing potential sources of resistance. By integrating these individuals into the system,

Kublai Khan aimed to create a sense of *shared governance*, albeit one heavily skewed in favor of Mongol authority.

Furthermore, Kublai Khan implemented policies aimed at encouraging economic **interdependence** between the conquered population and the Mongol ruling class. This included promoting trade and commerce, particularly along the revitalized Silk Road. Such economic incentives were designed to lessen the likelihood of rebellion and foster a sense of mutual benefit. However, this system also had its drawbacks. **Economic disparities** between Mongol elites and the Chinese population grew, leading to tensions and resentment.

The **religious policies** of Kublai Khan also played a significant role in his attempt to integrate the conquered territories. While his personal preference leaned towards Buddhism, he famously adopted a policy of religious tolerance, allowing for the coexistence of Buddhism, Taoism, Confucianism, Islam, and Christianity. This policy, while not without its limitations, aimed to lessen cultural friction and prevent religious conflict from becoming a catalyst for rebellion. Yet, religious freedom did not always translate into equal treatment, and certain religious groups faced greater challenges than others.

Ultimately, the **integration** of conquered territories and populations under Kublai Khan was a complex and often contradictory process. His approach was a blend of pragmatism and power, characterized by a willingness to adapt and incorporate elements of Chinese culture and administration while simultaneously maintaining the dominance of the Mongol ruling class. The long-term consequences of his policies, both successful and unsuccessful, shaped the *cultural and political landscape* of

China for centuries to come, leaving a lasting legacy of both cultural exchange and political tension.

Dealing with Resistance and Rebellion

The Consolidation of Power: A Necessary Brutality?

Kublai Khan's ascension to power and the subsequent establishment of the Yuan Dynasty were not without significant challenges. While his diplomatic skills and strategic acumen facilitated the expansion of his empire, the integration of conquered territories and diverse populations proved a far more arduous task. Resistance and rebellion, stemming from both internal and external sources, posed a constant threat to the stability of his rule, demanding swift and often ruthless responses. The Southern Song Dynasty's final collapse didn't signify the end of opposition; instead, it marked the beginning of a prolonged struggle for control and loyalty.

Internal Conflicts: Navigating Ethnic Tensions and Power Struggles

One of the most persistent challenges Kublai Khan faced was the management of internal dissent. The Mongol elite, accustomed to a decentralized system of power, often clashed with the Khan's centralized authority. Ambitious nobles and rival factions within the Mongol court frequently plotted against him, vying for influence and resources. This internal strife was further complicated by the delicate balance Kublai needed to maintain between the Mongol conquerors and the native Chinese population. He attempted to integrate both groups, but deep-seated cultural differences and historical prejudices frequently fueled conflicts and rebellions among the Han Chinese who often resented Mongol rule and the privileges bestowed upon their conquerors. The constant threat of internal rebellion forced Kublai to implement stringent security measures and a system of loyalist oversight which included harsh punishments for those suspected of disloyalty or rebellion.

External Threats: Maintaining Control Over a Vast Empire

Kublai Khan's empire stretched across a vast geographical expanse, encompassing diverse cultures, religions, and political systems. Maintaining control over such a sprawling territory presented formidable challenges. Border skirmishes and full-scale rebellions erupted in various parts of the empire, requiring constant military intervention. These uprisings, often fueled by ethnic tensions, religious differences, or local grievances against Mongol rule, tested the limits of the Yuan military's capabilities and stretched the empire's resources. The scale of some of these rebellions, particularly those in the south, demanded the deployment of significant military might and years of sustained campaigns to quell. The constant threat of external attack from neighboring states and resisting factions forced Kublai Khan to maintain a large and well-equipped army that continually shifted focus to suppress insurrections, diverting resources from other important aspects of governance.

Strategies for Suppression: A Multifaceted Approach

Kublai Khan employed a range of strategies to deal with resistance and rebellion, from diplomatic negotiations and concessions to outright military force. He attempted to win over some populations through patronage, religious tolerance, and economic incentives, but these measures were not always successful. His government attempted to create a balance of power, but the deep-seated tensions between different groups within the empire proved difficult to overcome. In some instances, he demonstrated **mercy** and forgiveness; in others, he resorted to <u>brutal</u> suppression. Massacres and punitive expeditions were not uncommon as he sought to maintain his authority and quell dissent forcefully.

The Legacy of Resistance: A Test of Imperial Power

The constant struggle against resistance and rebellion profoundly shaped the course of the Yuan Dynasty and Kublai Khan's reign. It forced him to allocate significant resources to military campaigns and internal security, potentially diverting funds from other projects that may have further improved the lives of his subjects. The need to consolidate power and maintain control also influenced his policies, leading to some practices that alienated parts of the population. While the Yuan Dynasty ultimately lasted for nearly a century, the repeated uprisings and rebellions served as a constant reminder of the fragility of even the most powerful empires. They tested the very limits of imperial power, highlighting the crucial and often brutal necessity of maintaining control in a vast and diverse realm.

Part II: Building the Yuan Dynasty

4. Establishing the Yuan Dynasty: A New Era

Formal establishment of the Yuan Dynasty

The formal establishment of the Yuan Dynasty in 1271 marked a pivotal moment in East Asian history, signifying not merely a change in rulers but a profound transformation of the political, social, and cultural landscape. Kublai Khan, having consolidated his power after years of relentless campaigns against the Song Dynasty, made the momentous decision to formally declare the founding of a new imperial dynasty, abandoning the title of Great Khan, which he previously held as the supreme ruler of the Mongol Empire, in favor of a title that resonated more deeply with the Chinese population. This was a carefully considered move, showcasing Kublai Khan's astute understanding of the need to integrate the conquered territories effectively and cultivate a sense of legitimacy among the Chinese subjects. The name "Yuan," signifying "origin" or "source," was chosen to emphasize a new beginning, aiming to signal a departure from the preceding Song Dynasty while implicitly claiming a position as the rightful successor to earlier Chinese dynasties.

The declaration was not a mere symbolic act; it was accompanied by a series of significant administrative and political reforms. Kublai Khan implemented a new administrative structure, drawing on aspects of both Mongol and Chinese systems. While retaining key Mongol officials in strategic positions, he also appointed numerous Chinese bureaucrats to critical administrative posts, ensuring a balance between preserving Mongol dominance and incorporating existing structures and expertise. This move, while pragmatic, also reflected a willingness to adapt and learn from the conquered territories, a key element in the long-term stability of the Yuan Dynasty.

The establishment of the Yuan Dynasty was further solidified by the construction of a new capital, Khanbaliq (modern-day Beijing). The city's strategic location, its grand scale, and the architectural grandeur of its palaces and temples served to underscore the power and authority of the new dynasty. The city became a melting pot of diverse cultures, attracting merchants and scholars from across Asia and Europe, contributing significantly to the unprecedented cultural exchange characteristic of Kublai Khan's reign. This cosmopolitan atmosphere, fostered deliberately by Kublai Khan's policies, enhanced the sense of a unified, albeit diverse, empire.

Beyond the administrative and symbolic aspects, the formal establishment of the Yuan Dynasty also marked the beginning of a distinct legal and economic framework. New laws and codes were introduced, although, these aimed at incorporating elements of both Mongol custom and Chinese legal traditions. This attempt at creating a comprehensive, cohesive system highlighted Kublai Khan's ambition to create a stable and enduring regime capable of governing the vast expanse of the empire effectively. The new legal system, though not without its flaws, provided a foundation upon which the Yuan would try to operate for almost a century.

In essence, the formal establishment of the Yuan Dynasty represented a *calculated* and ambitious undertaking by Kublai Khan. It was not simply a declaration of conquest, but rather a deliberate attempt to synthesize Mongol power with Chinese administrative traditions and cultural strengths, a bold strategy that would shape the future of the region for generations. The enduring impact of this decision is undeniable, as it dramatically altered the course of Chinese history and contributed significantly to the broader currents of world history. This moment reflects Kublai Khan's vision of a unified and prosperous empire, a vision that, despite its eventual limitations and the dynasty's eventual decline, fundamentally reshaped the political and cultural landscape of China.

The Yuan Dynasty, born from the ambition of one man, would leave an indelible mark on the tapestry of history, a legacy forged through conquest, adaptation, and a bold vision of a multi-cultural empire. Its significance extends far beyond the borders of China, showcasing a critical intersection between nomadic power and sedentary civilization.

Administrative Reforms and the Restructuring of the Government

Upon establishing the Yuan Dynasty, Kublai Khan faced the monumental task of governing a vast and diverse empire encompassing disparate cultures and administrative systems. His approach was pragmatic, recognizing the need to blend Mongol traditions with existing Chinese structures to create a stable and efficient administration. This wasn't a simple process of imposition but a complex negotiation between established practices and the demands of a newly formed imperial order.

One of the most significant changes introduced by Kublai Khan was the **restructuring of the central government.** He largely dismantled the complex Song bureaucracy, replacing it with a more streamlined system that reflected Mongol preferences for direct control. While borrowing elements from the established Chinese administrative frameworks, he consciously avoided mirroring them precisely, opting instead to build a structure more akin to the decentralized, militaristic nature of the Mongol Empire itself.

This involved **creating a new hierarchy** within the Yuan court, with prominent positions filled by both Mongols and loyal Chinese officials. This deliberate policy of inclusion aimed to balance the needs of the conquering power with the necessity of integrating the conquered population. This strategy, while successful to an extent, also sowed the seeds of future conflict.

The **creation of new administrative divisions** was another key element of Kublai Khan's reforms. The traditional Chinese provincial system, intricate and often inefficient in a vast empire, was modified to suit the Mongols' practical concerns. Provinces were often redefined to better reflect Mongol military and strategic considerations, resulting in a less geographically consistent pattern than its predecessor.

The legal system also underwent significant transformation. While retaining some aspects of Chinese law, Kublai Khan introduced a modified Yassa, the Mongol legal code, creating a hybrid system that attempted to reconcile the conflicting traditions. The application of this legal code varied across the empire, with different regions and communities experiencing differing levels of integration with the central legal authority.

Kublai Khan understood the **importance of economic management** in consolidating power. His reforms extended beyond administrative restructuring to include financial policies. He established a unified monetary system, replacing the diverse currencies previously in circulation, improving trade and facilitating economic interaction across the empire. This move demonstrated a keen understanding of the practical needs of governance, showing his attention to detail even within the large-scale processes of imperial administration.

Furthermore, the **appointment of officials** underwent a substantial shift. While competent Chinese administrators were retained, and indeed in some cases, elevated to important positions, loyalty to the Khan and the Yuan Dynasty was paramount. This required a delicate balancing act, as trust had to be earned from officials from vastly different cultural backgrounds, a challenge that Kublai Khan addressed through a combination of pragmatism and carefully applied power.

Ultimately, Kublai Khan's administrative reforms weren't simply about creating a new government; they were about **forging a new empire**. The successful integration of diverse populations and administrative systems within a single, unified framework was a key element of his legacy. His ability to blend Mongol and

Chinese administrative structures demonstrates a sophisticated understanding of governance and a willingness to adapt his policies to meet the unique needs of his immense and heterogeneous realm. The lasting impact of his efforts on China's administrative history is a testament to both his ambition and his political acumen.

The integration, however, was not without its flaws. The tension between Mongol and Chinese interests, woven into the fabric of the administrative system from the start, would ultimately contribute to the Yuan Dynasty's decline. The inherent challenges in reconciling such disparate elements within the same imperial structure ultimately manifested themselves over time, revealing the inherent complexities of Kublai Khan's lasting achievement.

Early Policies Towards the Chinese Population

Kublai Khan's approach to the Chinese population was a complex tapestry woven with threads of pragmatism, ambition, and inherent cultural clashes. His policies, far from being monolithic, evolved over time, reflecting both his strategic goals and the realities on the ground.

Initially, Kublai Khan adopted a relatively conciliatory stance. **He understood the need to win over the hearts and minds of the conquered populace** to ensure the stability of his new Yuan Dynasty. This was a departure from the often brutal tactics employed by earlier Mongol conquerors. <u>He actively sought the cooperation of prominent Chinese officials and scholars,</u> appointing many to key positions within the administration. This pragmatic approach aimed to leverage the existing bureaucratic expertise and networks of the Song Dynasty to facilitate efficient governance of his vast empire.

However, this initial tolerance didn't imply complete equality. While Chinese officials were employed, **they were largely subordinate to Mongol administrators and officials**. A clear hierarchical structure was maintained, with Mongols occupying the apex of power. This system, designed to maintain Mongol control, often led to resentment and friction among the Chinese elite, who felt their traditional authority and prestige had been diminished.

Kublai Khan's policies also reflected a degree of economic pragmatism. He recognized the importance of the Chinese economy to the sustenance and prosperity of the Yuan Dynasty. **He implemented policies to stimulate trade and agriculture**, recognizing that a flourishing Chinese economy would ultimately benefit the Mongol rulers. This economic engagement, however, was often accompanied by heavy taxation, which placed a significant burden on the Chinese population. While boosting the empire's coffers, this taxation fueled discontent and played a role in subsequent rebellions.

Furthermore, Kublai Khan's religious policies played a significant role in shaping his relations with the Chinese. *His promotion of Tibetan Buddhism as a state religion* was seen by many as an attempt to impose a foreign belief system upon the predominantly Confucian and Taoist Chinese population. While his policy of religious tolerance theoretically included other faiths such as Confucianism, Taoism, and Islam, the preferential treatment of Buddhism alienated some segments of Chinese society and contributed to growing cultural tensions.

In the later years of his reign, **Kublai Khan's policies towards the Chinese population became increasingly complex and inconsistent.** The initial conciliatory approach gave way to a more authoritarian style, partly driven by increased resistance and rebellions. Attempts to assimilate Chinese culture more fully into Mongol life were met with both success and failure. The increasing dominance of the Mongol aristocracy and the persistence of cultural differences ultimately hindered the seamless integration hoped for by Kublai Khan. This underscores the inherent complexities and contradictions inherent in attempting to rule such a vast and diverse population under a system that maintained a distinct separation of power based on ethnicity.

In conclusion, Kublai Khan's early policies towards the Chinese population were a **calculated blend of pragmatism and control.** While he sought to utilize Chinese expertise and economic strength, he maintained a fundamentally hierarchical system that prioritized Mongol dominance. This approach, while initially successful in establishing a stable empire, laid the seeds of future conflicts and ultimately contributed to the dynasty's eventual decline. His legacy serves as a compelling case study of the challenges and complexities of cross-cultural governance and empire building.

Challenges in Consolidating Power and Control

The establishment of the Yuan Dynasty under Kublai Khan, while a monumental achievement, was far from a smooth transition. Securing and maintaining control over such a vast and diverse empire presented a multitude of formidable challenges, testing the limits of even the most capable emperor.

One of the most significant hurdles was the inherent resistance to Mongol rule from the established Chinese elite. The Song Dynasty, despite its defeat, retained a strong cultural and intellectual influence, and many officials and scholars refused to cooperate with the new regime. This resistance manifested in various forms, from passive non-compliance to active rebellion and sabotage. Kublai Khan's attempts at **integration**, such as adopting certain aspects of Chinese administrative structures and appointing Chinese officials, were often met with skepticism and opposition. The deep-seated cultural differences and historical animosities between the Mongol conquerors and the conquered Chinese population created a fertile ground for discontent and unrest.

Furthermore, the sheer **scale** of the Yuan Empire posed a logistical nightmare. Maintaining effective communication and control across such vast distances presented a significant challenge. While the extensive network of roads and canals helped, it was inadequate to address the vastness of the territory. News of rebellions, administrative failures, and economic fluctuations would often reach the capital in Khanbaliq long after the events themselves, making swift and decisive action difficult. This geographical expanse also exacerbated problems of resource allocation and tax collection, further weakening central authority.

The Yuan Empire's **multi-ethnic composition** also created immense challenges for Kublai Khan. Balancing the interests of various ethnic groups – Mongols, Chinese, Persians, and others – proved exceedingly difficult. Favoritism shown towards one group invariably led to resentment and hostility from others, creating a complex web of internal rivalries and power struggles. Maintaining a cohesive governing structure and preventing ethnic tensions from escalating into open conflict demanded constant vigilance and skillful diplomacy, often tested beyond its limits.

The **economic policies** implemented by Kublai Khan, while ambitious, also faced significant challenges. Attempts to integrate the diverse economic systems of the conquered territories and boost trade along the Silk Road were occasionally met with resistance and unforeseen difficulties. Maintaining a stable currency and a functioning tax system across such a vast and heterogeneous population was a constant struggle, often leading to widespread inflation and economic hardship.

Internal **power struggles** within the Mongol court further destabilized the empire. Competition among Kublai Khan's relatives and advisors for influence and power often erupted into open conflict, undermining the emperor's authority and diverting crucial resources from essential governance tasks. These internal conflicts not only weakened the central government, but also provided opportunities for rebellions and uprisings in the provinces.

Finally, **military campaigns**, while expanding the empire's reach, also placed significant strains on its resources. The costly expeditions to Japan and Southeast Asia, though ultimately unsuccessful, diverted substantial funds and manpower from internal administration and infrastructure development, leaving the empire vulnerable to both internal and external threats. The burden of maintaining a massive standing army and equipping and supplying it across such vast distances proved an immense and continuous strain on the empire's treasury.

In conclusion, Kublai Khan faced numerous obstacles in consolidating his power and controlling his vast empire. The resistance of the Chinese elite, the logistical challenges of governing such a large territory, the complexities of managing a multi-ethnic population, and the strains of ambitious economic and military policies all contributed to a volatile and precarious situation. Despite his many accomplishments, maintaining absolute control remained an ongoing and ultimately incomplete challenge throughout his reign.

5. The Capital of Khanbaliq: A City of Empires

Planning and construction of the new capital

The construction of Khanbaliq, Kublai Khan's new capital, represents a monumental undertaking reflecting his ambition and vision for the Yuan Dynasty. More than simply a city, it served as a potent symbol of the empire's power and its ambition to integrate Mongol and Chinese cultures. The planning process was likely complex, involving a collaboration of Mongol engineers and architects with experienced Chinese urban planners. The location itself, strategically situated at the heart of his vast empire, was chosen for its accessibility, proximity to vital trade routes, and existing infrastructure.

While precise details remain elusive due to the limited surviving documentation, historical accounts and archaeological evidence suggest a meticulously planned city. The construction was likely a massive project, employing a vast workforce comprising both skilled artisans and laborers from diverse backgrounds. The city's layout, based on a grid system—a hallmark of Chinese urban planning—was designed to ensure efficient administration and ease of navigation. This blended with the Mongol preference for spaciousness and functionality. The use of traditional Chinese building techniques and materials can be seen in surviving structures and depictions of the city, indicating a high degree of integration between the two cultures.

The grand scale of Khanbaliq is evidenced by its size and the monumental architecture within its walls. The imperial palace, a sprawling complex, served as the heart of the Yuan court. Its design undoubtedly reflected Mongol tastes, showcasing expansive courtyards and halls. However, the integration of elements of Chinese architecture, particularly in the use of timber and intricate ornamentation, shows a willingness to embrace and synthesize diverse cultural influences. The city also contained elaborate temples, bustling markets, and residential areas, catering to a diverse population that spanned ethnicities and social strata.

The construction of Khanbaliq extended over many years, demanding significant resources and manpower. The immense undertaking may have faced logistical and technical challenges, such as sourcing building materials and coordinating labor. However, the success of the project showcases the efficiency and administrative capabilities of the Yuan Dynasty under Kublai Khan. The city's very existence stands as a testimony to his determination to construct a lasting legacy. The city's layout, blending Mongol practicality with Chinese urban planning expertise, illustrates Kublai Khan's adeptness at harnessing different cultures and skills in the service of his grand vision.

The construction of Khanbaliq was not merely a feat of engineering; it was a powerful statement of cultural integration. The city served as a living testament to Kublai Khan's ambitions. It was a hub for trade, a center of political power, and a melting pot of cultures, all contained within its walls. The carefully planned layout, the integration of architectural styles, and the diversity of its population, all point to a deliberate attempt to create a new, unified identity for his expanding empire. The creation of Khanbaliq thus transcends the simple construction of a city; it reflects the complex and ambitious objectives of Kublai Khan's reign. It stands as a symbol of his pursuit to bridge the gap between Mongol traditions and the rich cultural heritage of China.

Archaeological discoveries continue to shed light on the intricacies of Khanbaliq's planning and construction. The ongoing research helps us further appreciate the scale and complexity of the endeavor. These findings not only add to our understanding of the city's physical development but also shed light on the societal and cultural dynamics of the Yuan Dynasty. Ultimately, Khanbaliq serves as a tangible representation of Kublai Khan's far-reaching ambitions and his enduring legacy within the annals of world history.

Architectural Influences and Cultural Blending in Khanbaliq

The construction of Khanbaliq, Kublai Khan's magnificent capital, stands as a powerful testament to the cultural synthesis that defined his reign. It wasn't merely a city; it was a living embodiment of the Yuan Dynasty's unique blend of Mongol pragmatism and Chinese sophistication.

The city's layout, a deliberate fusion of Mongol nomadic traditions and established Chinese urban planning, reflects this intriguing interplay. Unlike rigidly structured Chinese cities, Khanbaliq embraced a more organic design. Vast, open spaces catered to the Mongols' equestrian lifestyle, while meticulously planned districts housed the diverse populace. The city's radial street pattern, a departure from the traditional grid system, allowed for efficient movement and provided ample room for the sprawling imperial palaces and temples.

Architectural styles presented a similarly fascinating collage of influences. While traditional Chinese pavilion-style buildings, with their ornate roofs and sweeping eaves, formed the backbone of many structures, they were adapted and modified to suit Mongol preferences. **Mongol yurts**, initially temporary dwellings, inspired the design of certain palatial structures, incorporating their circular forms and the use of portable sections for flexibility. This wasn't mere imitation but rather a conscious integration, transforming familiar forms to serve new functions and reflect a new imperial identity.

The use of materials further exemplifies this cultural fusion. While **Chinese artisans** contributed their expertise in brickwork, carpentry, and intricate ornamentation, Mongol architects embraced materials such as wood and felt, reflecting their nomadic heritage. The incorporation of these diverse materials into palatial architecture wasn't accidental; it signaled a deliberate policy of *cultural inclusion* and a symbolic unification of distinct aesthetic traditions.

Beyond the practical aspects of design and construction, the choice of **architectural styles** also carried significant symbolic weight. The blending of Chinese and Mongol styles was not just aesthetic but also political. It served to legitimize Kublai Khan's rule in the eyes of both his Mongol subjects and the Chinese population. The grand scale and imperial magnificence of Khanbaliq aimed to project an image of power and stability, unifying the diverse populations under a common banner.

Furthermore, religious structures within Khanbaliq exemplify this cultural melting pot. Buddhist temples, Taoist shrines, and even Christian churches found their place in the city, reflecting Kublai Khan's policy of religious tolerance. The architectural styles of these religious buildings reveal their various origins, yet they coexist peacefully, demonstrating the harmonious integration of faith within the cosmopolitan city. This tolerance extended to artistic expression, as seen in the city's diverse sculptures, paintings, and decorative arts, each showcasing the cultural richness of the empire.

In conclusion, the architecture of Khanbaliq stands as a vivid manifestation of the successful cultural exchange that defined the Yuan Dynasty under Kublai Khan. It wasn't merely a capital city but a physical embodiment of his vision: a vibrant metropolis where diverse cultures intersected and flourished, leaving an indelible mark on the architectural landscape and the cultural heritage of China. The city remains a powerful symbol of cultural blending and successful imperial integration, demonstrating the remarkable capacity of human societies to adapt, innovate, and build something new from diverse sources.

The City's Role as a Hub for Trade and Cultural Exchange

Khanbaliq, the magnificent capital city constructed by Kublai Khan, transcended its role as a mere seat of power; it blossomed into a vibrant nexus of global trade and unprecedented cultural fusion, a testament to the emperor's ambitious vision and shrewd policies.

Strategically situated, Khanbaliq (modern-day Beijing) became a pivotal intersection on the Silk Road, inheriting and expanding upon the legacy of previous trading networks. Kublai Khan understood the immense economic potential of facilitating commerce, actively promoting the free flow of goods and people across his vast empire and beyond. This fostered an era of unprecedented prosperity, enriching not only the Yuan Dynasty's coffers but also the lives of its citizens and fostering a dynamic exchange of ideas and technologies.

The city's infrastructure played a crucial role in its success as a trading hub. Vast networks of roads and canals, meticulously constructed and maintained under Kublai Khan's reign, facilitated the efficient transport of goods over long distances. This intricate system significantly reduced travel times and costs, attracting merchants from across Eurasia and beyond. The city's layout itself, a masterful blend of Mongol and Chinese architectural styles, reflected this spirit of integration.

Khanbaliq was not just a conduit for material goods; it also became a melting pot of cultures. Merchants brought with them not only their wares but also their customs, languages, and religious beliefs. The city hosted diverse communities, representing a wide spectrum of ethnicities and faiths. The presence of Muslim, Christian, Buddhist, and Taoist communities within the city's walls showcased Kublai Khan's policy of religious tolerance. This fostered a climate of intellectual curiosity and cultural exchange, leading to an unprecedented level of interaction and synthesis among disparate cultures.

The **interaction between cultures** in Khanbaliq was not merely a passive phenomenon; it led to significant innovations and cross-cultural pollination. Architectural styles, artistic techniques, philosophical ideas, and scientific advancements were shared and adapted, creating a truly unique cultural landscape. The fusion of Mongol pastoral traditions with Chinese agricultural practices, for example, profoundly impacted the Yuan Dynasty's economy and society.

Marco Polo's famous accounts provide valuable insights into the dynamism of Khanbaliq. He described a city teeming with life, where merchants from distant lands traded exotic goods, artists created stunning works of art, and scholars engaged in lively intellectual debates. His vivid descriptions paint a portrait of a cosmopolitan city, brimming with energy and brimming with diversity, unlike anything seen in Europe at that time. The volume of trade generated by this bustling metropolis generated vast wealth, strengthening the Yuan empire and fueling its growth.

However, the success of Khanbaliq as a trading hub was not without its challenges. Managing such a diverse population and balancing the interests of different groups required political skill and diplomacy. Yet, Kublai Khan's shrewd leadership and relatively tolerant policies ensured that Khanbaliq remained a beacon of commerce and cultural exchange, a shining example of the potential for harmonious interaction among diverse peoples in a vast empire.

In conclusion, Khanbaliq's role as a central hub for trade and cultural exchange was a defining feature of Kublai Khan's reign and a testament to his visionary leadership. The city's success highlights the benefits of fostering international commerce and the positive outcomes of embracing cultural diversity. Its legacy continues to resonate today, serving as a reminder of the powerful forces of globalization and the enduring impact of a ruler who understood and harnessed their potential.

Economic Growth and Development under Kublai Khan's Reign

Kublai Khan's reign witnessed a period of significant economic expansion and development within the Yuan Dynasty, a testament to his pragmatic approach to governance and his understanding of the crucial role of economic prosperity in maintaining a stable and powerful empire.

The economic policies implemented during Kublai Khan's rule were characterized by a degree of pragmatism and innovation that distinguished them from his predecessors. He recognized the need to integrate the diverse economies of the conquered territories into a cohesive whole, fostering a system that facilitated both internal trade and international commerce. This involved a multifaceted approach, encompassing infrastructure development, fiscal reforms, and a deliberate promotion of trade along the Silk Road and beyond.

One of the most impactful initiatives undertaken during his reign was the ambitious program of **infrastructure development**. The construction of extensive networks of canals and roads dramatically improved transportation and communication across the vast Yuan Empire. These infrastructure projects not only facilitated the movement of goods but also stimulated economic activity along their routes, fostering the growth of towns and villages. The *Grand Canal*, a vital artery of the Chinese economy, received significant attention and investment, further enhancing its capacity to transport grain and other commodities throughout the empire.

Beyond infrastructure, Kublai Khan implemented key fiscal reforms aimed at streamlining the tax system and promoting economic stability. He introduced a more efficient system of tax collection, reducing corruption and enhancing the government's ability to finance its ambitious projects. His emphasis on stability created a more predictable economic environment, encouraging investment and fostering growth. He understood the importance of balancing the needs of the state with the interests of merchants and traders, creating an atmosphere conducive to economic expansion.

Perhaps the most enduring contribution to economic growth under Kublai Khan was the revival and expansion of trade along the Silk Road. He recognized the crucial role of trade in generating wealth and fostering cultural exchange. His policies actively encouraged merchants from across Eurasia to conduct business within the Yuan Empire, resulting in a period of unprecedented prosperity. The Silk Road flourished under his rule, becoming a major conduit for the exchange of goods, ideas, and technologies, connecting the East and West in a vibrant network of commercial activity. This boosted the Yuan economy by generating significant revenue through customs duties and taxes and stimulating the growth of various industries across the empire.

The **economic policies** of Kublai Khan were not without their challenges. The vast size of the empire presented administrative hurdles, and ensuring the fair and efficient distribution of resources across diverse regions required considerable effort and attention. Yet, his overall commitment to economic growth is undeniable, leading to the growth of cities, an increase in overall wealth, and the establishment of trade links across the world. He fostered an environment of relative stability and prosperity that enabled the Yuan Dynasty to flourish economically, at least for a significant period.

In conclusion, Kublai Khan's reign was marked by a remarkable period of economic growth and development. His investment in infrastructure, implementation of fiscal reforms, and promotion of trade, especially along the Silk Road, transformed the economic landscape of the Yuan Dynasty, establishing the foundation for considerable prosperity and leaving a lasting legacy of economic innovation. His rule stands as a prime example of how strategic economic planning and a pragmatic approach to governance can drive economic expansion and contribute to the strength and stability of an empire.

6. Economic Reforms and Infrastructure Projects

The Implementation of New Economic Policies

Kublai Khan's reign witnessed a profound restructuring of the Yuan Dynasty's economic landscape, marked by innovative policies designed to consolidate power, foster prosperity, and integrate the diverse territories under his rule. These reforms, while bearing the hallmarks of Mongol pragmatism, also drew upon existing Chinese administrative traditions and sought to harmonize them with the empire's unique circumstances.

One of the most significant changes was the reorganization of the tax system. The previous system, inherited from the Song Dynasty, often proved inefficient and inequitable. Kublai Khan introduced a more centralized approach, standardizing taxation across different regions and simplifying the collection process. This was crucial in generating a steady revenue stream for the vast empire, enabling the ambitious infrastructure projects and military campaigns that characterized his reign. While aiming for fairness, the system still faced challenges in accurately assessing land values and effectively collecting taxes from diverse populations, leading to occasional instances of unrest and resistance.

The **promotion of trade** formed another cornerstone of Kublai Khan's economic policy. He understood the crucial role of commerce in enriching the empire and fostering cultural exchange. The **Silk Road**, already a vital trade route, experienced a period of unprecedented flourishing under his patronage. New roads and canals were constructed, connecting distant regions and facilitating the movement of goods and people. This increased connectivity led to a significant increase in the volume of trade, enriching both the imperial coffers and the merchants involved. The influx of foreign goods and ideas, particularly from the West, contributed significantly to the burgeoning cosmopolitan culture of Khanbaliq (modern-day Beijing).

Furthermore, Kublai Khan implemented policies aimed at stimulating *agricultural production*. He invested heavily in irrigation projects and land reclamation schemes, aiming to increase the yields of crops crucial to feeding the empire's massive population. These efforts, while showing some success, faced constraints due to factors like climate variability and logistical challenges across the vast empire. Incentives were offered to farmers, encouraging greater agricultural output and stability, although the effects were not uniformly positive across all regions.

The **introduction of paper money** represented another significant innovation, reflecting the growing complexity of the Yuan economy. While paper currency existed before, Kublai Khan's reforms aimed to standardize and regulate its use. This move facilitated large-scale transactions and eased the burden of transporting vast quantities of coinage. However, the system was not without its drawbacks. The uncontrolled printing of paper money at times led to inflation and economic instability. Managing the monetary supply proved to be a complex challenge, demonstrating the inherent difficulties in implementing such large-scale economic reform.

Finally, the Yuan Dynasty saw the development of a more sophisticated <u>system of banking and finance</u>. This involved the establishment of state-sponsored banks and the expansion of private lending institutions. These institutions played a crucial role in facilitating trade, providing credit to merchants, and managing the flow of capital within the empire. This development represented a significant advancement in financial systems, although it also created opportunities for exploitation and corruption, which the administration struggled to control effectively.

In conclusion, Kublai Khan's economic policies represented a complex interplay of Mongol administrative approaches, Chinese traditions, and innovative solutions to the challenges of governing a vast and diverse empire. While some policies yielded substantial successes in stimulating trade and generating revenue, others, like managing the paper currency, presented significant hurdles. The overall impact, however, underscores his ambition to create a prosperous and integrated empire, a testament to his vision and lasting legacy.

Development of Infrastructure such as Canals and Roads

A Legacy Etched in Stone and Water:

Kublai Khan's reign witnessed a remarkable expansion of infrastructure, fundamentally reshaping the Yuan Dynasty's landscape and economy. This wasn't merely a matter of military logistics; it represented a conscious strategy to unite the vast empire, facilitate trade, and bolster the prosperity of his diverse subjects. The construction of **canals** and **roads** became cornerstones of his ambitious vision, directly impacting the lives of millions across China and beyond.

The **Grand Canal**, a pre-existing marvel of engineering, underwent significant improvements and extensions under Kublai Khan's orders. He oversaw crucial repairs, expanded its reach to connect more regions, and implemented efficient management systems to ensure its continuous operation. This wasn't simply about maintaining existing infrastructure; it was about **strategically enhancing its capacity** to transport grain, goods, and troops across the empire's heartland. The efficient movement of grain, for instance, was essential in preventing famines and maintaining social stability – a key element in the longevity of any dynasty.

Beyond the Grand Canal, Kublai Khan's administration initiated the construction of a **vast network of roads**, some paved with stone, others meticulously maintained earthen tracks. These roads weren't just haphazard paths; they were **carefully planned arteries** connecting major cities, facilitating both domestic and international trade. The **Silk Road**, already a crucial trade route, flourished under his rule, directly benefiting from the improved infrastructure. The increased flow of goods and people brought economic prosperity and spurred cultural exchange across Eurasia. The improved roads also played a critical role in military operations, allowing for quicker troop movements and facilitating a more responsive response to rebellions or external threats.

These ambitious infrastructural projects required enormous resources and manpower. *The mobilization of labor* for these projects provides a fascinating window into the Yuan administration. While some historians highlight the potential for exploitation and hardship faced by laborers, others point to the creation of jobs and economic opportunities, emphasizing the multiplier effect of such large-scale undertakings. The resulting network of canals and roads not only improved trade and transportation but also facilitated the movement of people, ideas, and cultural practices, **contributing to a unique blend of Mongol and Chinese culture**.

The legacy of Kublai Khan's infrastructure improvements is undeniable. Even after the Yuan Dynasty's fall, many of the canals and roads remained in use, continuing to shape the economic and social geography of China for centuries to come. The improved transport links fostered regional integration, strengthened the empire's economic base, and facilitated cultural exchange, leaving an enduring impact on the history of East Asia and the wider world. His policies illustrate the profound ways in which physical infrastructure can shape the trajectory of an empire, influencing not just its economic power, but its social stability and cultural identity. The **strategic planning and execution** behind these projects underscore Kublai Khan's visionary leadership and his understanding of how infrastructure could be leveraged to build a stable and prosperous empire.

The construction of canals and roads under Kublai Khan represents more than simply bricks and mortar; it stands as a powerful symbol of his vision for a unified and prosperous empire, a testament to his ability to integrate diverse populations, and a lasting legacy visible even today.

Promotion of trade along the Silk Road

A Golden Age of Commerce Under Kublai Khan

Kublai Khan's reign witnessed a **remarkable flourishing** of trade along the Silk Road, a testament to his astute economic policies and strategic vision. He understood the vital role commerce played in consolidating power, enriching his empire, and fostering cultural exchange across vast distances. Unlike some of his predecessors who focused primarily on military conquest, Kublai Khan recognized the *transformative potential of economic prosperity* to unite his diverse empire and enhance its global standing.

One of his key strategies was the **systematic improvement of infrastructure**. The Silk Road, a network of ancient trade routes, was not merely a geographical concept but a vital artery of the empire. Kublai Khan ordered extensive repairs and improvements to existing roads, bridges, and caravanserais (roadside inns). This ensured the safe and efficient passage of merchants and their goods, significantly reducing travel times and associated risks. The **construction of new roads and canals**, particularly within China, further facilitated trade and connected previously isolated regions.

Beyond infrastructure, Kublai Khan implemented *progressive economic policies* that encouraged trade. He implemented a relatively stable monetary system, promoting the use of paper money and standardizing weights and measures across the empire. This simplification of economic transactions significantly reduced uncertainty and encouraged both domestic and international trade. He also **lowered trade taxes** in many areas, making the Silk Road even more attractive to merchants from diverse backgrounds.

The **policy of religious tolerance** adopted by Kublai Khan also played a crucial role in fostering trade.

Merchants from various religious and cultural backgrounds felt safe and welcome within the Yuan Empire, contributing to a more vibrant and inclusive commercial environment. This contrasted sharply with previous eras where religious differences often led to conflict and hampered trade.

Kublai Khan's court actively **promoted trade partnerships** with various countries and regions. He established diplomatic relations and trade agreements with many nations, ensuring the safe passage of goods and the protection of merchants' interests. This proactive approach towards international trade significantly increased the volume and diversity of goods flowing along the Silk Road.

The **impact of Kublai Khan's policies on the Silk Road** was profound. It experienced a golden age, facilitating unprecedented exchange of goods, ideas, and technologies between East and West. From precious silks and spices to porcelain and advanced technologies, the Silk Road facilitated a vast flow of commodities, enriching the economies of both the Yuan Dynasty and the wider world. *This period of prosperity* would significantly shape the cultural landscape of Eurasia for centuries to come.

However, it's important to note that the **Silk Road's flourishing wasn't without its challenges**. Maintaining peace and security along the vast trade routes required significant military investment, and the empire faced internal rebellions and external threats that occasionally disrupted trade. Despite these difficulties, the overall effect of Kublai Khan's policies was a remarkable increase in commercial activity and cultural exchange.

In conclusion, Kublai Khan's deliberate promotion of trade along the Silk Road stands as a testament to his insightful leadership and pragmatic approach to governance. By prioritizing infrastructure development, implementing sound economic policies, fostering religious tolerance, and actively pursuing international trade partnerships, he **transformed the Silk Road into a powerful engine of economic growth and cultural exchange**, leaving an enduring legacy of prosperity and interconnectedness.

The Impact of Economic Policies on the Empire's Prosperity

Kublai Khan's reign, while marked by significant military achievements and cultural exchanges, was fundamentally shaped by his economic policies. These policies, a complex interplay of innovation and adaptation, profoundly influenced the prosperity—and ultimately the stability—of the vast Yuan Empire. Understanding their impact requires examining not only their immediate effects but also their long-term consequences on the economic and social fabric of the empire.

One of the most crucial aspects of Kublai Khan's economic strategy was the **revitalization of the Silk Road**. He understood the vital role of trade in fueling economic growth, and he actively invested in infrastructure improvements to facilitate commerce. The construction and maintenance of roads, canals, and bridges, along with the establishment of secure trade routes, significantly reduced transport costs and travel time, boosting both domestic and international trade. This led to a surge in economic activity, enriching both the empire's coffers and the lives of its citizens. The influx of goods and ideas from across Eurasia enriched the Yuan culture and stimulated innovation in various sectors.

Beyond infrastructure, Kublai Khan implemented **innovative monetary policies**. The standardization of currency, the introduction of paper money on a large scale, and the establishment of a robust banking system greatly eased transactions and facilitated economic transactions. These reforms, although not without their challenges (like inflation during certain periods), significantly stimulated economic activity and contributed to the overall prosperity of the empire. The stability provided by a functioning financial system attracted both domestic and foreign investment, further fueling economic growth.

However, Kublai Khan's economic vision wasn't solely focused on trade and finance. He also recognized the importance of **agricultural development**. Investments in irrigation projects, land reclamation schemes, and agricultural technologies greatly increased crop yields, ensuring food security for the burgeoning population. This focus on agricultural productivity not only prevented widespread famine but also provided a surplus that could be channeled into other sectors of the economy. This ensured stability and contributed to the empire's overall prosperity, providing a strong base for urban development and trade.

The **integration of diverse economic systems** was another defining characteristic of Kublai Khan's economic policies. The Yuan Empire encompassed a vast array of cultures and economic systems, from the established agricultural economies of China to the nomadic pastoralism of the Mongols. Rather than imposing a uniform system, Kublai Khan adopted a pragmatic approach, adapting and integrating different economic practices. This fostered a dynamic and diverse economy, allowing for specialization and innovation across various regions.

Yet, the long-term effects of Kublai Khan's economic policies remain a subject of debate. While his reforms undeniably brought a period of relative prosperity, questions remain about the extent of that prosperity and its distribution across different segments of the population. Some historians argue that the benefits were primarily enjoyed by the elite and urban centers, while others emphasize the significant improvements in the lives of ordinary citizens. The subsequent decline of the Yuan Dynasty also raises questions about the sustainability of its economic model in the long run. Was the prosperity achieved through sustainable methods, or were there inherent flaws in the system that ultimately contributed to its downfall? These are complex questions requiring further historical analysis and investigation.

In conclusion, Kublai Khan's economic policies were a cornerstone of his reign, profoundly shaping the prosperity of the Yuan Empire. His investments in infrastructure, his innovative monetary reforms, his focus on agricultural development, and his pragmatic approach to integrating diverse economic systems all contributed to a period of significant economic growth. However, a balanced assessment demands a critical examination of both the immediate and long-term consequences of these policies, their impact on different social strata, and the reasons for the ultimate economic and political decline of the dynasty.

Part III: Cultural Exchange and Foreign Relations

7. Marco Polo's Journey: A Venetian at the Court of Khan

Marco Polo's Arrival in the Yuan Court

*The year is likely 1271. A young Venetian, **Marco Polo**, embarked on a journey that would etch his name into the annals of history. His arrival at the court of **Kublai Khan**, the fifth Khagan of the Mongol Empire and founder of the Yuan dynasty, wasn't a mere accidental encounter; it was the culmination of a perilous and arduous expedition across continents, driven by a potent mix of ambition, curiosity, and perhaps, a touch of youthful audacity.*

Precise details surrounding Polo's initial reception remain shrouded in some historical ambiguity. Accounts vary, often colored by the passage of time and the lens through which the narrative is presented. What is certain, however, is that his arrival was not an insignificant event.

The Mongol court, a vibrant tapestry of diverse cultures and influences, was a nexus of power and intrigue, a microcosm of the vast empire it represented. **Kublai Khan**, known for his shrewd intellect and strategic thinking, was unlikely to overlook the arrival of a Westerner, especially one who, according to Polo's own writings, possessed an engaging personality and a willingness to learn and adapt.

The journey itself, a testament to the tenacity of the Polo family and their companions, serves as a compelling backdrop to the story of their arrival. The Silk Road, a network of trade routes stretching across Eurasia, was not merely a geographical pathway; it was a cultural conduit, a bridge connecting civilizations that had long remained relatively isolated. The Polos' traversal of this route, fraught with challenges and encounters with disparate peoples and customs, undoubtedly enriched their experiences and perspectives, setting the stage for their interactions with the sophisticated and cosmopolitan court of the Yuan Dynasty.

Imagine the scene: a retinue of weary travelers, bearing gifts that would reflect both their Venetian heritage and their journey's length, approaching the imposing structures of Khanbaliq (present-day Beijing), the capital city. The vastness of the city itself – a marvel of urban planning, blending elements of Mongol and Chinese architecture – must have been overwhelming. The sheer scale of **Kublai Khan's** empire, evident even in its capital city, was a dramatic introduction to the power and influence of the Mongol leader.

The details of their first audience with **Kublai Khan** are lost to time, but we can reasonably assume a level of formality and protocol consistent with Mongol court etiquette. **The initial interaction** likely involved the exchange of gifts, an assessment of the travelers' credentials, and perhaps a demonstration of their adaptability and willingness to serve the Khan. It is highly probable that *Polo's linguistic skills, his familiarity with trade routes, and his adaptability played a pivotal role* in determining his reception at court.

The subsequent years would solidify **Marco Polo's** position within the Yuan court. His service under **Kublai Khan**, encompassing various diplomatic and administrative roles, offered him unique access to the inner workings of the empire. This firsthand experience, meticulously recorded in his later writings, became the foundation of our understanding of the Yuan Dynasty, offering a vital, albeit sometimes controversial, perspective on one of history's most expansive and influential empires.

Therefore, **Marco Polo's arrival** at the Yuan court was not merely a geographical event; it was a pivotal moment in the intercultural exchange between East and West, a convergence of civilizations that forever altered the course of history and continues to fascinate and inspire us today. His journey, and his subsequent service in the court, provided a unique opportunity for cultural understanding and cross-cultural dialogue, a narrative that continues to shape our understanding of a pivotal era.

The **impact** of this meeting resonates through history, shaping perceptions of the Mongol Empire and leaving a lasting legacy in the realm of global exploration and intercultural communication. It is a testament to the complex interplay of individual agency and historical forces, underscoring the enduring power of exploration, adaptability, and the seemingly insignificant moments that can have world-altering consequences.

His service under Kublai Khan and his observations

Marco Polo's service under Kublai Khan, lasting nearly two decades, provided him with unparalleled access to the heart of the Yuan Dynasty. His observations, meticulously recorded and later immortalized in his famous travelogue, offer a rich and multifaceted perspective on the emperor, his court, and the vast empire he ruled.

Far from a simple narrative of exotic encounters, Polo's account reveals a keen eye for detail and a shrewd understanding of the political, economic, and social structures of the Yuan Dynasty. His descriptions of Khanbaliq (present-day Beijing), the imperial capital, paint a vivid picture of a cosmopolitan city teeming with people from diverse backgrounds, a testament to Kublai Khan's policy of cultural exchange and religious tolerance. Polo's detailed descriptions of the city's layout, architecture, and bustling marketplaces provide invaluable insights into the urban planning and economic prosperity of the era.

Beyond the grandeur of the capital, Polo's observations extend to the broader workings of the Yuan administration. He describes the **efficient postal system**, the extensive network of roads and canals, and the sophisticated system of taxation and governance that underpinned the empire's stability and growth. These details, often overlooked in other historical accounts, underscore the *sophistication of Yuan administration* and its significant achievements in infrastructure development.

His role within the imperial court afforded Polo unique access to the emperor himself. He portrays Kublai Khan as a far-sighted and ambitious ruler, keenly interested in expanding trade, improving infrastructure, and consolidating his power. Polo's narrative reveals Kublai Khan's interest in foreign affairs and his willingness to engage with emissaries from different parts of the world. The description of the Khan's interactions with Polo and other foreign dignitaries illustrates his openness to diverse cultures and his efforts to foster international relations. The descriptions of trade missions, diplomatic envoys, and the sheer volume of goods circulating through the empire, all underscore Kublai Khan's successful promotion of global trade and the empire's role in facilitating the Silk Road's prosperity.

Moreover, Polo's account doesn't shy away from presenting a more nuanced picture of Yuan rule. He notes instances of oppression, rebellion, and the challenges faced in managing such a diverse and sprawling empire. His observations about the complex relationship between Mongol rulers and the Chinese population, while colored by his own perspective, provide valuable insights into the dynamics of imperial rule. He doesn't simply glorify the Khan; rather, he offers a more nuanced and realistic portrayal, acknowledging the strengths and weaknesses of the empire's governance.

In conclusion, Marco Polo's observations, though filtered through his own experiences and biases, remain an invaluable source for understanding the Yuan Dynasty under Kublai Khan. His detailed accounts of the imperial court, the economic and political structures of the empire, and the interactions between different cultures contribute significantly to a deeper and more comprehensive understanding of this pivotal period in Chinese and world history. His perspective not only highlights the significant achievements of Kublai Khan's reign but also reveals the complexities and challenges inherent in governing such a vast and diverse realm.

The Impact of Polo's Accounts on the Western World's Perception of the East

Marco Polo's travels and subsequent recounting in his famous book, Il Milione (The Million), profoundly reshaped the Western world's understanding of the East, an impact that continues to resonate even today. Before Polo's narrative, the East – specifically the vast and mysterious lands of the Mongol Empire – was largely a realm of legend, rumor, and fantastical tales. His firsthand account, while not without its inaccuracies and embellishments, offered a degree of concrete detail and tangible experience that irrevocably altered European perceptions.

Prior to Polo's writings, knowledge of the East in Europe was primarily filtered through religious texts, travelers' tales of dubious authenticity, and second-hand accounts. These sources often depicted the East as a place of exotic wonders, but also of danger, mystery, and often, barbarity. The Orient was frequently presented as a land of unimaginable riches and splendor, but also as a place fraught with peril, populated by monstrous beings and powerful, enigmatic rulers. Polo's narrative, while still containing elements of the exotic and the fantastical, presented a more grounded, albeit still somewhat romanticized, picture.

One of the most significant impacts of Polo's account was the introduction of a more detailed understanding of the Mongol Empire and its administration. He described

Kublai Khan's court, its opulence, and its surprisingly sophisticated bureaucracy. This challenged the existing European notion of the Mongols as simply savage hordes. While Polo's narrative still emphasized the power and military might of the Mongols, it also revealed the complexity of their governance, their impressive infrastructure, and their vast trade networks. This portrayal, however partial, offered a more nuanced understanding than previous accounts, fostering a more complex – and in some ways, less fearsome – image of this vast empire.

Furthermore, Polo's descriptions of Eastern cities like Khanbaliq (present-day Beijing) and its bustling markets, advanced technologies, and diverse populations profoundly altered European perceptions of urban life in the East. He painted a picture of cosmopolitan centers that rivaled, and in some cases surpassed, the sophistication of European cities. This countered the prevailing European view that placed Europe at the cultural and technological apex of the world. The sheer scale and wealth of the East, as detailed by Polo, were awe-inspiring, sparking further curiosity and a desire for exploration.

However, it is crucial to acknowledge that Polo's account also perpetuated certain stereotypes and misconceptions. While he introduced a more detailed view of the East, his descriptions were still filtered through a European lens, and his account inevitably reflected the biases of his time. Some of his descriptions were exaggerated or embellished, and he lacked a deep understanding of many Eastern customs and practices. Despite these limitations, his narrative sparked a European fascination with the East, inspiring further exploration and laying the groundwork for increased trade and cultural exchange in the centuries to come.

The enduring legacy of Marco Polo's account lies not merely in its factual accuracy, but in its ability to ignite the imagination of European readers. It served as a catalyst for a new era of exploration and discovery, fueling the voyages of later explorers like Christopher Columbus and Vasco da Gama, who were, in part, inspired by the tales of Polo's adventures. While the accuracy of his details has been debated for centuries, the broader impact of Polo's work on the Western world's understanding of and relationship with the East is undeniable. His account, while imperfect, fundamentally shifted the European perception of Asia from a hazy land of myth and legend to a more tangible, if still partially enigmatic, region filled with diverse cultures, immense wealth, and untold possibilities.

In conclusion, Marco Polo's account, despite its inevitable biases and inaccuracies, stands as a pivotal moment in the shaping of Western perceptions of the East. It moved the East from the realm of fantasy into a more concrete, albeit still partially misunderstood, reality, setting the stage for centuries of interaction and exchange between East and West. This legacy continues to be felt, as scholars continue to analyze and interpret his account, revealing both the enduring power of storytelling and the complexities of intercultural exchange throughout history.

Assessing the Accuracy of Polo's Accounts

The enduring fascination with Marco Polo's Travels, and its depiction of Kublai Khan's court, necessitates a critical examination of its veracity. While undeniably influential in shaping Western perceptions of the East, the accuracy of Polo's accounts remains a subject of ongoing scholarly debate.

One major point of contention centers around the sheer scale and detail of Polo's descriptions. He paints a vivid picture of a vast and sophisticated empire, detailing its cities, customs, and governance with impressive specificity. **Skeptics** argue that the level of detail, particularly concerning the advanced technologies and administrative systems described, is inconsistent with the available independent historical evidence. Some scholars suggest that Polo's account might be embellished or even partially fabricated, potentially influenced by existing tales of the Orient prevalent in Europe at the time.

Conversely, **proponents** of Polo's accuracy point to corroborating evidence found in other contemporary sources. Although limited, these sources, including accounts from other travelers and official documents from the Yuan dynasty, support certain aspects of Polo's narrative. The existence of Khanbaliq (modern-day Beijing), the descriptions of trade routes like the Silk Road, and references to specific customs and practices find resonance in these independent records. This lends credence to the overall plausibility of Polo's journey and his immersion in Yuan society, albeit perhaps not in the exact level of detail he provides.

Another critical factor in evaluating Polo's accuracy is his *perspective*. As a Venetian merchant, his observations were naturally filtered through his own cultural lens and experiences. His descriptions often emphasize aspects of the Yuan court that would be of interest to a European audience – trade, wealth, political structures – while potentially overlooking or minimizing other important facets of Yuan life. This bias inherently limits the objectivity of his account and must be carefully considered during analysis.

Moreover, **the translation and transmission** of Polo's account also introduce elements of uncertainty. The original text, written in a medieval Venetian dialect, has undergone numerous translations and adaptations over the centuries. These processes inevitably introduce variations and interpretations, potentially influencing the interpretation of specific events or descriptions. Thus, comparing modern versions of *The Travels* demands close attention to the scholarly lineage of each translation and its potential biases.

Recent scholarship emphasizes the **importance of context** when assessing Polo's claims. Instead of focusing solely on proving or disproving specific details, researchers are increasingly using the account as a window into the perceptions and interactions of East and West during this crucial historical period. The narrative provides valuable insights into the intercultural exchange, the economic realities of the Silk Road, and the functioning of the Yuan government, albeit through a distinctly biased European lens.

In conclusion, while the complete accuracy of Marco Polo's *Travels* remains a complex and contested issue, dismissing the account entirely would be a mistake. By acknowledging its limitations – including potential embellishments, translational biases, and the inherent limitations of a single perspective – scholars can still extract valuable insights into the life of Kublai Khan and the dynamics of his vast and complex empire. The work serves as a significant historical document, not necessarily as a perfectly factual chronicle, but as a critical testament to the power of cultural exchange and the enduring impact of a single eyewitness account on the imagination of the West.

8. Religious Tolerance and Cultural Synthesis

Kublai Khan's Policy of Religious Tolerance

A cornerstone of Kublai Khan's reign and a significant departure from some of the more religiously homogeneous policies of previous Mongol leaders, his embrace of religious pluralism was a calculated strategy with profound implications for the stability and prosperity of his vast empire.

Unlike some of his predecessors who favored a singular religious tradition, Kublai Khan actively cultivated a policy of **religious tolerance**. This wasn't merely passive acceptance; it was an **active promotion** of different faiths within the Yuan Dynasty. His court became a melting pot of diverse religious beliefs, a testament to his pragmatic understanding that fostering religious harmony could be instrumental in uniting his diverse populace. This approach contrasted sharply with the sometimes forceful religious conversions seen in other historical empires.

The **practical benefits** of this policy were numerous. By allowing the free practice of various religions—including Buddhism, Taoism, Confucianism, Islam, and Christianity—Kublai Khan skillfully prevented the religious conflicts that could have destabilized his already complex and multicultural empire. This policy also served to attract talent and expertise from diverse communities, enriching his court and administration. Scholars, artists, and administrators, regardless of their religious affiliation, found a welcoming environment under his rule. The vibrant exchange of ideas that resulted from this religious openness contributed significantly to the cultural and intellectual flourishing of the Yuan Dynasty.

His personal approach to religion also played a significant role. While Kublai Khan showed a particular affinity for Tibetan Buddhism, **he did not impose it upon his subjects.** His patronage of Buddhist institutions and monasteries was extensive, but it coexisted alongside his support for other religious traditions. He demonstrated a remarkable ability to navigate the complexities of religious practice, displaying a genuine respect for diverse spiritual paths rather than merely tolerating their existence.

The impact of Kublai Khan's religious policies extended beyond the immediate sphere of his court. The relatively peaceful coexistence of different religious communities fostered a sense of **social cohesion** and stability, particularly in regions where religious tensions had previously been high. This facilitated economic development and cultural exchange, leading to a period of relative prosperity and growth throughout much of the Yuan Dynasty. The vibrant religious landscape of the era is vividly illustrated by the presence of numerous temples, mosques, and churches across the empire, standing as silent witnesses to Kublai Khan's unique approach to governance.

However, it's crucial to acknowledge that while Kublai Khan's policy promoted tolerance, **it wasn't without its limitations.** Religious freedom wasn't always absolute, and the extent of tolerance varied across different regions and time periods within his reign. Certain religious groups may have faced restrictions, and the emperor's personal preferences undoubtedly influenced the allocation of resources and patronage among different faiths. Nevertheless, the overall impact of his policies on the religious landscape of the Yuan Dynasty was transformative, fostering an environment of religious pluralism that would leave a lasting mark on Chinese history.

In conclusion, Kublai Khan's policy of religious tolerance wasn't simply a matter of pragmatic governance; it represented a significant shift in imperial policy, reflecting a nuanced understanding of the diverse social and cultural fabric of his empire. This calculated strategy, characterized by active promotion of various faiths, played a crucial role in consolidating his power, fostering economic growth, and enriching the cultural tapestry of the Yuan Dynasty. His legacy as a champion of religious pluralism remains a striking feature of his reign, setting a precedent that would be studied and debated for centuries to come.

The Coexistence of Buddhism, Taoism, Confucianism, Islam, and Christianity

Kublai Khan's reign, a pivotal moment in Eurasian history, was marked by a remarkable degree of **religious tolerance**. Unlike many rulers who enforced a single state religion, Kublai fostered a climate where *Buddhism, Taoism, Confucianism, Islam, and Christianity* could coexist, albeit with varying degrees of official patronage. This policy, a striking departure from the often-violent religious conflicts of the era, reflected Kublai's pragmatic approach to governance and his understanding of the diverse beliefs of his vast empire.

Buddhism, particularly the Tibetan form, enjoyed significant favor under Kublai. He actively supported the construction of temples, monasteries, and the translation of Buddhist scriptures. The Dalai Lama's lineage was strengthened during his reign, with significant political and spiritual influence exerted by Tibetan Buddhist leaders within the Yuan court. This patronage wasn't simply a matter of religious preference but also a shrewd political move, as Buddhism's emphasis on peace and order resonated with the emperor's desire for stability within his multi-ethnic empire.

Taoism, with its deep roots in Chinese culture, continued to thrive alongside Buddhism. While not receiving the same level of overt imperial support as Buddhism, Taoist practices and beliefs remained influential among the Chinese population. Kublai Khan, a shrewd political leader, understood the importance of maintaining harmony with pre-existing belief systems, recognizing that directly supplanting native religions could lead to instability.

Confucianism, with its emphasis on social hierarchy and moral order, played a crucial role in administering the Yuan Dynasty. Although not directly promoted as a state religion, Confucian scholars continued to hold positions of power, especially in bureaucratic administration. Kublai Khan recognized the pragmatic value of Confucian principles in managing the vast bureaucracy necessary to govern his sprawling empire. This pragmatic approach underscores the multifaceted nature of Kublai's religious policies – he didn't simply tolerate different faiths but utilized their strengths strategically for effective governance.

The presence of **Islam** within the Yuan Dynasty, largely due to the significant Muslim population in Central Asia and parts of China, was readily accepted. Muslim communities maintained their religious practices and played vital roles in trade and administration. Many Islamic scholars and merchants flourished under the Yuan's relatively tolerant policies. This suggests an element of both tolerance and strategic recognition of the economic and social contributions made by the Muslim communities to the Yuan's prosperity.

The arrival of **Christianity**, primarily through Nestorian Christians who had already established a presence in China for centuries, was another significant element of the religious landscape. While not a dominant faith, Christianity received a measure of tolerance, reflecting the wide-ranging scope of Kublai's religious acceptance. This tolerance underscores his willingness to accept a variety of religious traditions within the bounds of his expansive empire.

Kublai Khan's policy of religious tolerance wasn't simply a matter of benign indifference. It was a calculated strategy rooted in his pragmatic approach to governance and an understanding that religious harmony was essential for maintaining stability in his multicultural empire. The coexistence of these diverse faiths, while not without its internal complexities, contributed to a unique and vibrant cultural landscape during the Yuan Dynasty, demonstrating the emperor's remarkable ability to foster unity within diversity.

Note: While tolerance was practiced, this doesn't imply complete equality among faiths. The level of official patronage and social influence varied considerably across the religious traditions, often reflecting political and strategic considerations. However, the relative peace and freedom of practice enjoyed by these multiple faiths under the rule of Kublai Khan remains a noteworthy aspect of his legacy.

Patronage of the arts and cultural exchange

Kublai Khan's reign, while marked by significant military achievements and political maneuvering, also witnessed an unprecedented flourishing of arts and cultural exchange within the Yuan Dynasty. His patronage wasn't merely a display of imperial power; it was a deliberate strategy to consolidate his rule and forge a unique cultural identity for his multi-ethnic empire. This policy of cultural synthesis fostered an environment where diverse artistic traditions intermingled, resulting in a vibrant and innovative creative landscape.

One of the most striking aspects of Kublai Khan's patronage was his embrace of diverse artistic styles. While he appreciated traditional Chinese art forms, he also actively encouraged the integration of Mongol, Persian, and even Western artistic influences. This resulted in a unique blend of styles seen in architecture, painting, sculpture, and literature. The construction of Khanbaliq (present-day Beijing), his new capital, exemplifies this policy. The city's architecture, a fusion of Mongol nomadic aesthetics and Chinese imperial grandeur, served as a physical manifestation of his vision of a unified empire. This monumental undertaking involved mobilizing vast resources and diverse skilled artisans from across his empire, a testament to his ability to harness creative talent for imperial purposes.

Beyond architecture, Kublai Khan's patronage extended to painting and calligraphy. He commissioned numerous works from both Chinese and foreign artists, resulting in a rich collection reflecting a wide spectrum of artistic styles. These artworks often featured themes of imperial power, landscapes reflecting the vastness of his empire, and depictions of court life, all contributing to the creation of a visual narrative of the Yuan Dynasty. The patronage of calligraphy, particularly within the imperial court, ensured the continued development and refinement of this highly esteemed art form, reflecting both the emperor's personal interest and the importance he placed on literary culture.

The Silk Road, during the Yuan Dynasty, served not only as a vital trade route but also as a conduit for the exchange of artistic ideas and techniques. Kublai Khan's active promotion of trade facilitated the movement of artists and artisans across Eurasia, leading to a cross-pollination of artistic styles and innovations. This is evident in the introduction of new materials, techniques, and aesthetic sensibilities into Chinese art, while simultaneously contributing to the wider dissemination of Chinese artistic traditions throughout the Mongol empire and beyond.

The emperor's patronage also extended to the performing arts. Court ceremonies and theatrical performances, featuring both traditional Chinese and Mongol elements, were lavish affairs intended to both entertain and impress. These events further served to reinforce the imperial authority and project an image of cultural dominance. Music, dance, and dramatic performances played an integral role in shaping the court culture and influencing artistic trends throughout the wider empire.

Beyond the visual and performing arts, Kublai Khan also showed a keen interest in literature. He sponsored the translation of foreign texts into Chinese, making these works accessible to a wider audience. This fostered intellectual exchange and broadened the horizons of Chinese scholars. Conversely, he also encouraged Chinese literary works to be translated into other languages, furthering the dissemination of Chinese culture and ideas throughout his vast empire.

Kublai Khan's patronage of the arts was not a haphazard endeavor; it was a carefully considered policy designed to legitimize his rule and build a sense of shared cultural identity within his multi-ethnic empire. By fostering a vibrant and inclusive artistic landscape, he sought to unify his diverse subjects under a common cultural banner. The legacy of his patronage continues to resonate today, visible in the rich tapestry of artistic styles and cultural expressions that emerged during the Yuan Dynasty, demonstrating the enduring power of imperial patronage in shaping a nation's cultural heritage.

The *success* of Kublai Khan's strategy of cultural synthesis is evident in the lasting influence of Yuan art and culture. The blending of artistic traditions resulted in a unique style that continues to inspire and inform artists today. His reign stands as a remarkable example of how imperial patronage can not only enrich a nation's cultural landscape but also contribute to the creation of a cohesive and unified society, bridging cultural divides in an era of unprecedented global interconnectedness.

The Development of a Unique Yuan Cultural Identity

Kublai Khan's reign, while marked by significant military conquests and administrative reforms, witnessed a profound and **unprecedented cultural synthesis**. The Yuan Dynasty, far from being a mere imposition of Mongol culture upon China, fostered a unique blend of Mongol, Chinese, and other Eurasian traditions, resulting in a vibrant and distinct cultural identity. This wasn't a passive merging, but rather a dynamic interplay of influences, shaped by Kublai Khan's deliberate policies and the inherent dynamism of intercultural exchange.

One of the key factors contributing to this unique cultural identity was Kublai Khan's policy of **religious tolerance**. Unlike previous conquerors who often suppressed indigenous faiths, Kublai Khan actively promoted the coexistence of Buddhism, Taoism, Confucianism, Islam, and Christianity. This resulted in a remarkable level of religious pluralism, where different faiths not only coexisted but also influenced one another, enriching the overall cultural landscape. The construction of magnificent temples and monasteries, showcasing diverse architectural styles, served as physical manifestations of this religious harmony. The *tolerance extended beyond religion*, encompassing aspects of art, literature, and daily life, promoting a sense of inclusivity and mutual respect among diverse communities.

Furthermore, the Yuan Dynasty witnessed a significant **patronage of the arts**. Kublai Khan, himself a cultured individual, actively supported artists and scholars from various backgrounds. This resulted in a flourishing of artistic creativity, incorporating elements of Mongol nomadic art, refined Chinese aesthetics, and influences from Central Asia and the Middle East. The resulting artistic creations reflected this unique blend of styles, creating a distinctly Yuan aesthetic that was simultaneously cosmopolitan and deeply rooted in the diverse cultural traditions of the empire. Paintings, sculptures, ceramics, and textiles all bear testament to this extraordinary cultural fusion, offering a visual record of this remarkable era.

The establishment of **Khanbaliq (present-day Beijing)** as the capital city played a pivotal role in shaping Yuan culture. Designed as a cosmopolitan metropolis, it drew together people from across the vast empire, creating a melting pot of cultures. The city's architectural landscape reflected this diversity, combining elements of Mongol yurts and traditional Chinese palatial structures. The bustling marketplaces of Khanbaliq showcased a remarkable array of goods from across the Silk Road, further contributing to the cultural exchange and the development of a unique Yuan identity. This urban center became a symbol of the empire's power and a catalyst for cultural interaction, facilitating the exchange of ideas, artistic styles, and daily practices.

The **administrative structure** itself contributed to the synthesis of cultures. While maintaining a core Mongol leadership, Kublai Khan consciously integrated Chinese officials and administrators into the government. This resulted in a hybrid administrative system that combined Mongol efficiency with Chinese bureaucratic expertise. This integration extended beyond the administrative sphere, impacting various aspects of societal governance, law, and daily life. The interaction between Mongol and Chinese administrative practices resulted in innovations and adaptations that reflected the unique needs and characteristics of the Yuan Dynasty.

Despite the significant presence of Mongol elites, the Yuan Dynasty saw a **remarkable degree of cultural exchange and adaptation**. The Mongol language and customs did not entirely supplant those of the Chinese population, instead coexisting and influencing one another. The result was a fusion of traditions, with Mongol elements becoming integrated into daily Chinese life and vice versa. This complex interaction wasn't always harmonious, but it did result in a uniquely blended cultural identity that distinguishes the Yuan Dynasty as a particularly vibrant and influential period in Chinese history.

In conclusion, the Yuan Dynasty under Kublai Khan did not simply represent the dominance of one culture over another. It fostered a unique cultural identity through a remarkable blend of Mongol and Chinese, as well as other Eurasian traditions. This synthesis was shaped by policies promoting religious tolerance, patronage of the arts, cosmopolitan urban planning, and the strategic integration of administrative systems. This dynamic interplay of cultural forces resulted in a legacy that continues to resonate through the centuries, highlighting the enduring power of intercultural exchange and the complex interplay of power and cultural adaptation.

9. Foreign Relations and Diplomacy: Expanding Influence

Diplomatic Missions and Embassies to Other Empires

Kublai Khan's reign witnessed a sophisticated and multifaceted diplomatic network extending far beyond the borders of his vast Yuan Empire. His strategy transcended mere conquest, prioritizing strategic alliances and fostering trade relationships to solidify his power and influence on the world stage. This section delves into the intricate web of diplomatic missions and embassies that characterized his rule, revealing a keen understanding of international relations and a remarkable ability to navigate the complex political landscape of 13th-century Eurasia.

One of the most crucial aspects of Kublai Khan's foreign policy was the establishment of regular diplomatic exchanges with neighboring states and distant empires. These missions served multiple purposes, ranging from securing trade agreements and solidifying alliances to gathering intelligence and projecting an image of Yuan strength and prestige. The frequency and scale of these missions were unprecedented, reflecting Kublai Khan's ambitious vision of a globally interconnected empire.

Among the most notable diplomatic endeavors were those directed towards the **Islamic world**. Kublai Khan sent numerous envoys to various Islamic states, including the *Mamluk Sultanate of Egypt*, the *Ilkhanate* in Persia, and the *Golden Horde* in Russia. These missions often involved the exchange of gifts, the negotiation of trade agreements, and the discussion of political matters. The success of these diplomatic initiatives is evident in the establishment of relatively peaceful and productive relationships between the Yuan and these powerful Islamic entities, facilitating trade and cultural exchange along the Silk Road.

The East Asian diplomatic landscape also received considerable attention. Kublai Khan engaged in extensive diplomacy with the remaining Song Dynasty, attempting negotiation even as military campaigns continued. He also pursued relations with the various kingdoms of Southeast Asia, seeking alliances and trading partnerships. These diplomatic missions highlight Kublai Khan's strategic vision, which recognized the importance of securing stability and economic prosperity within the East Asian sphere of influence. The goal was not merely domination but the integration of these diverse states into a system mutually beneficial to the Yuan and its neighbors.

Beyond Eurasia, Kublai Khan's ambition extended towards establishing contact with Europe. While the legendary voyages of **Marco Polo** are well-documented, they were part of a broader strategy of reaching out to Western powers. Though direct diplomatic relations with European states were limited, Kublai Khan's interest in Europe demonstrates a global outlook that was far ahead of its time. His attempts to establish links with the West showcase an understanding that extending his influence required not only military might but also skillful diplomacy and international cooperation.

The effectiveness of Kublai Khan's diplomatic efforts was mixed. While some missions resulted in lucrative trade agreements and solidified alliances, others encountered resistance or outright hostility. The failure to fully subdue the Southern Song Dynasty and the unsuccessful attempts to conquer Japan serve as reminders that diplomacy, even when skillfully executed, does not always guarantee success. However, the sheer scale and scope of Kublai Khan's diplomatic initiatives underscore his ambition and his remarkable understanding of the importance of international relations in shaping the destiny of his vast empire.

The legacy of Kublai Khan's diplomatic missions extends far beyond his reign. His efforts fostered trade and cultural exchange across Eurasia, contributing to the prosperity of the Silk Road and the exchange of ideas and innovations among diverse cultures. The intricate network of embassies he established stands as a testament to his political acumen and his vision of a unified and prosperous world.

In conclusion,

Kublai Khan's diplomatic endeavors were a critical component of his governance, demonstrating a sophisticated understanding of international relations and highlighting his ambition to forge a unified and prosperous Eurasia. The sheer scale and scope of his diplomatic initiatives, combined with his willingness to engage with diverse cultures, cemented his place as a significant figure in world history, shaping the political and economic landscape of the 13th century and beyond. His legacy serves as a powerful reminder of the crucial role diplomacy plays in shaping the destinies of empires and nations.

Trade agreements and alliances with foreign powers

Kublai Khan's reign witnessed a complex tapestry of **foreign relations**, shaped by strategic alliances, lucrative trade agreements, and the ever-present need to maintain stability within his vast and diverse empire. His approach wasn't solely about military conquest; it was a nuanced blend of diplomacy, economic pragmatism, and the recognition that prosperity often stemmed from mutually beneficial partnerships.

One of the most significant aspects of Kublai Khan's foreign policy was his *active pursuit of trade relations*. The **Silk Road**, already a vital artery of commerce, flourished under his rule. He understood the economic power inherent in connecting distant markets and facilitating the flow of goods, ideas, and cultures. This wasn't simply a matter of economic self-interest; it was a strategic move to integrate his empire into a global network, forging dependencies and enhancing his influence on the world stage. Specific trade agreements were established with various states, encompassing everything from the exchange of luxury goods – silks, spices, porcelain – to the trade of essential resources vital for the Yuan's economic strength. These agreements went beyond simple bartering; they involved complex negotiations, the establishment of trade routes, and the protection of caravans to ensure the safe passage of merchants and their goods. The economic prosperity brought about by these agreements was essential to his long reign and the stability of the empire.

Beyond trade, Kublai Khan actively **forged alliances** with various powers. This was often a strategic response to perceived threats or a calculated means of expanding his sphere of influence. His diplomatic efforts weren't confined to the immediate neighbors of the Yuan Dynasty; they extended to distant lands, reflecting a sophisticated understanding of international politics. These alliances were multifaceted, sometimes involving royal marriages to consolidate power, while in other instances they entailed joint military operations against common enemies, or the exchange of ambassadors to maintain open lines of communication and foster goodwill. The careful construction and maintenance of these alliances were pivotal to Kublai's ability to manage the multiple challenges posed by internal unrest and external threats. He understood that securing powerful allies could significantly reduce the likelihood of conflicts, or provide a crucial buffer should conflict become unavoidable.

The establishment of diplomatic missions to distant lands underscores Kublai Khan's strategic vision. These missions were not just symbolic gestures; they were proactive efforts to establish direct contact with other empires and kingdoms, creating pathways for trade, political maneuvering, and the exchange of information. The willingness to send diplomatic envoys, often traveling vast distances across challenging terrains, speaks volumes about the importance that Kublai placed on maintaining peaceful relationships and developing strong external connections.

However, Kublai Khan's foreign policy wasn't always successful. His attempts to conquer Japan, for example, ended in disastrous failure due to a combination of unfavorable weather conditions and strong Japanese resistance. This highlights the limitations of even the most powerful empire and underscores the unpredictable nature of international relations. Even with carefully constructed alliances and lucrative trade agreements, unexpected events and the inherent complexities of global power dynamics could ultimately disrupt Kublai Khan's ambitious plans. The lessons learned from these failures however, would influence future strategies and negotiations, demonstrating his capacity for both ambitious plans and insightful learning.

In conclusion, Kublai Khan's foreign policy was a sophisticated blend of diplomacy, trade, and strategic alliances. While not without its failures, it played a crucial role in shaping the Yuan Dynasty's prosperity and global influence. His legacy illustrates the importance of both military might and effective diplomacy in managing a vast empire and navigating the complex landscape of international relations. The trade agreements and alliances established under his rule left an indelible mark on the economic and political landscape of Eurasia, influencing trade routes, fostering cultural exchange and shaping the course of history for centuries to come.

Attempts to expand influence beyond the existing borders

Kublai Khan's ambition extended far beyond consolidating his rule over China. His relentless pursuit of power propelled him towards ambitious expansionist policies, aiming to solidify the Yuan Dynasty's dominance across Asia and potentially beyond. These attempts, while ultimately meeting with mixed success, significantly shaped the political landscape of the 13th century and left an enduring mark on history.

One of Kublai Khan's most significant foreign policy objectives was the conquest of Japan. Driven by a desire to extend the Mongol Empire's reach across the East Asian sea, he launched two major invasions in 1274 and 1281. These expeditions, though boasting impressive logistical feats, ultimately *failed* due to a combination of factors: fierce resistance from the Japanese samurai, unfavorable weather conditions (including powerful typhoons, later romanticized as "divine winds"), and the logistical challenges of sustaining a large army across the sea. The failure to subdue Japan represented a significant setback to Kublai Khan's expansionist dreams, highlighting the limitations of even the most powerful empire when facing determined resistance and the unpredictable forces of nature.

In contrast to the Japanese campaigns, Kublai Khan enjoyed more success in his interactions with Southeast Asia. His expansionist efforts in this region were primarily driven by a desire to control vital trade routes and secure access to valuable resources. He successfully established tributary relationships with various kingdoms in the region, such as Annam (Vietnam), Champa, and Burma. These interactions weren't always peaceful; military campaigns were undertaken to enforce tributary status or to quell rebellious factions. While direct rule was not always established, Kublai Khan's influence extended significantly throughout Southeast Asia through a complex network of diplomacy, trade, and strategic alliances, thereby enriching the Yuan Dynasty's coffers and broadening its geopolitical reach.

Beyond military conquest and diplomacy, Kublai Khan also sought to expand influence through the promotion of trade. He understood the importance of the **Silk Road** and invested heavily in maintaining and improving the infrastructure that supported this vital artery of commerce. The increased flow of goods and cultural exchange along these trade routes not only boosted the Yuan Dynasty's economy but also fostered the dissemination of Yuan culture and ideas across a vast geographic expanse. This "soft power" approach to expansion proved to be more sustainable and ultimately more impactful than purely military means in the long run. By promoting trade and cultural exchange, Kublai Khan established a far-reaching network of influence that extended beyond the formal boundaries of his empire.

Kublai Khan's attempts to expand the Yuan Dynasty's influence beyond its existing borders were multifaceted, employing military force, diplomatic strategies, and economic initiatives. While his ambition was ultimately curtailed by setbacks in Japan and other challenges, his efforts profoundly impacted the political, economic, and cultural landscape of 13th-century Asia and beyond. His reign serves as a compelling case study in the complex interplay of military might, diplomatic skill, and economic policy in shaping the rise and fall of empires. The legacy of these attempts continues to resonate in the intricate historical tapestry of the region, underscoring the enduring power of ambition and the complexities of imperial expansion.

-A Conclusive Note-

Conflicts with neighboring states and empires

Kublai Khan's reign, while marked by significant expansion and consolidation, was not without its external conflicts. The vastness of the Yuan Empire and its ambitions inevitably led to clashes with neighboring powers, testing the limits of Mongol military might and diplomatic prowess.

One significant conflict involved **Japan**. Kublai Khan, aiming to extend his dominion across the seas, launched two major invasions in 1274 and 1281. These ambitious expeditions, however, ended in devastating defeats for the Yuan forces. Typhoons, known as *kamikaze* ("divine winds"), played a crucial role in thwarting the Mongol fleets, contributing to a lasting sense of Japanese national identity forged in the face of foreign aggression. The failure of these invasions not only checked the expansion of the Yuan Empire but also demonstrated the limitations of even the most powerful military when facing unexpected environmental factors and determined resistance.

In **Southeast Asia**, Kublai Khan's ambitions also met with resistance. His interactions with the **kingdoms of Annam (Vietnam) and Champa** involved a mixture of diplomacy and military campaigns. While the Mongols achieved some measure of success in establishing tributary relationships, complete subjugation proved elusive. These conflicts highlighted the challenges of projecting power across diverse geographical and cultural landscapes. The logistical complexities and the fierce resistance of local populations presented formidable obstacles to the Yuan's ambition for complete regional dominance. These campaigns, although partially successful in expanding Yuan influence, consumed significant resources and manpower, impacting the empire's overall stability.

Further west, the Yuan Empire's borders frequently rubbed against those of other powerful entities. **The Ilkhanate**, a Mongol khanate in Persia, experienced periods of both cooperation and tension with Kublai Khan's Yuan Dynasty. Succession disputes and shifting alliances within the Mongol world occasionally led to border skirmishes and competition for resources. While largely avoided through skillful diplomacy, the potential for conflict always loomed. These internal tensions within the wider Mongol sphere underscored the challenges of maintaining unity and coordinating policies across a vast and fragmented empire.

Kublai Khan's interactions with the **Mamluk Sultanate of Egypt** also represent a significant facet of his foreign policy. While direct military conflict was avoided, the two powers engaged in a complex dance of diplomacy and espionage. The Mamluks, having decisively defeated a Mongol army at Ain Jalut in 1260, posed a formidable barrier to further Mongol expansion westward. This stalemate signified the ultimate limit of Kublai Khan's territorial ambitions in the Middle East. It also underscores the growing strength of established powers that actively resisted Mongol advances.

The conflicts detailed above demonstrate that while Kublai Khan's reign was characterized by unparalleled expansion, it was also punctuated by persistent external challenges. His attempts to further extend Yuan control encountered stiff resistance from established kingdoms and the unpredictable forces of nature. These encounters reveal not only the military capabilities of the Yuan Empire but also the complex interplay of geopolitics, military strategy, diplomacy, and cultural differences that shaped the destiny of the Yuan Dynasty and its interactions with the surrounding world. The *successes and failures* on these different fronts ultimately contributed to the shaping of the Yuan Dynasty's legacy and its lasting impact on East Asia and beyond.

Part IV: Challenges and Legacy

10. The Limits of Imperial Power: Internal Conflicts

Rebellions and uprisings within the empire

The vastness and diversity of Kublai Khan's empire, a testament to his ambition and military prowess, simultaneously presented a formidable challenge to his authority. While the Yuan Dynasty enjoyed periods of relative stability and prosperity, it was far from immune to the constant threat of rebellion and uprising. These internal conflicts, stemming from a multitude of factors, ultimately tested the limits of imperial power and contributed significantly to the dynasty's eventual decline.

One of the primary sources of unrest was the inherent tension between the Mongol ruling class and the Chinese population. Despite Kublai Khan's efforts to integrate the two cultures, deep-seated resentment lingered. The Mongols, often perceived as foreign conquerors, imposed their own legal system and social hierarchy, often disregarding or overriding existing Chinese traditions and structures. This led to widespread discontent, fueling various uprisings, particularly among those who clung to the traditions of the former Song Dynasty.

Furthermore, the economic policies implemented by the Yuan court, while aiming to boost the empire's prosperity, sometimes proved detrimental to specific segments of the population. The imposition of new taxes, coupled with the disruption of traditional economic activities, triggered widespread hardship and resentment in various regions. This economic hardship frequently acted as a catalyst for rebellious movements, as desperate people took up arms against what they perceived as an oppressive regime.

Religious and ethnic differences also contributed to the instability within the empire. The Yuan Dynasty, while officially adhering to a policy of religious tolerance, still witnessed conflicts between different religious groups. These conflicts, often fueled by ethnic tensions, frequently escalated into widespread violence and rebellion, challenging the stability of the empire.

The scale and frequency of these rebellions varied throughout Kublai Khan's reign. Some were relatively localized, easily suppressed by the Yuan's powerful military. Others, however, proved far more challenging, threatening to destabilize entire provinces or even the empire itself. The Red Turban Rebellion, a particularly significant uprising, proved to be a harbinger of the Yuan Dynasty's ultimate downfall, demonstrating the inherent fragility of an empire built upon conquest and the persistent challenges of governing a vast and diverse population.

The responses of the Yuan government to these uprisings also varied. In some instances, Kublai Khan opted for a relatively lenient approach, attempting to appease the rebels through concessions or negotiated settlements. In others, he unleashed the full force of the Mongol military, resorting to brutal suppression and widespread massacres in an attempt to restore order. This inconsistent approach, often influenced by the specifics of each rebellion, underscores the complexity of governing such a vast and diverse empire.

The legacy of these internal conflicts is undeniable. They significantly weakened the Yuan Dynasty, diverting resources from crucial infrastructure projects and economic initiatives. The constant need to suppress rebellions strained the imperial treasury and depleted the military's manpower, leaving the empire vulnerable to further internal and external threats. Ultimately, the countless rebellions and uprisings during Kublai Khan's reign served as a stark reminder of the inherent challenges in maintaining control over a vast and diverse empire built on conquest, and highlight the crucial role internal dissent played in the eventual decline and fall of the Yuan Dynasty.

The frequency and intensity of these uprisings underscore the inherent difficulties of governing such a vast multi-ethnic empire. The Yuan Dynasty's ultimate inability to effectively address these internal conflicts stands as a cautionary tale for future empires, highlighting the critical interplay between effective governance, cultural sensitivity, and economic stability in maintaining a unified and prosperous state. The challenges faced by Kublai Khan in quelling these uprisings offer valuable insight into the complex dynamics of empire building and the inherent fragility of even the most powerful states.

Challenges in Managing a Vast and Diverse Empire

The monumental task of governing the sprawling Yuan Dynasty presented Kublai Khan with unprecedented challenges. His empire, a patchwork of diverse cultures and ethnicities stretching across continents, demanded a delicate balance of power, diplomacy, and effective administration – a feat that proved both exhilarating and excruciatingly difficult.

The sheer scale of the Yuan Dynasty was a primary hurdle. Unlike previous dynasties confined largely to China, Kublai Khan's domain encompassed vast territories from modern-day Korea to Persia, encompassing a breathtaking array of landscapes, climates, and peoples. Maintaining effective communication and control across such distances presented a logistical nightmare. Messages could take months to travel between provinces, and the swift suppression of rebellions or the efficient distribution of resources relied heavily on a well-maintained infrastructure and a loyal, efficient bureaucracy – both of which were constantly tested.

The cultural diversity within the empire posed an equally significant challenge. The Yuan Dynasty was a fusion of Mongol, Chinese, and numerous other cultures. While Kublai Khan demonstrated an appreciation for and practiced a policy of religious tolerance, fostering a degree of cultural exchange, this coexistence wasn't without friction. Deep-seated prejudices and historical antagonisms between different ethnic groups often flared into open conflict. The Mongols, as the ruling elite, often found themselves alienated from the Chinese populace, who harbored resentment toward their conquerors. This created a volatile atmosphere, with the potential for widespread uprisings and rebellions that frequently threatened the stability of the empire.

The integration of conquered territories and populations into the Yuan administrative system was another major challenge. Kublai Khan implemented various policies aimed at integrating the conquered Chinese population, including the adoption of Chinese administrative practices, the promotion of Chinese officials, and the implementation of a unified legal code. However, the Mongol rulers often maintained a distinct administrative structure and social hierarchy, which perpetuated tensions and prevented true cultural fusion. The system created inherent imbalances, leading to resentment among the Chinese and further challenges in unifying the diverse populations under one rule.

Furthermore, the economic management of such a vast empire proved immensely complex. The Yuan Dynasty relied heavily on trade along the Silk Road, but maintaining secure trade routes and managing the flow of goods and resources over such immense distances required significant investment in infrastructure and a highly developed logistics system. This was exacerbated by various natural disasters, climate changes and periodic famines, which frequently disrupted supply chains and led to social unrest. The economic disparity between various regions also added to the administrative burden, making it extremely difficult to ensure equitable distribution of wealth and resources.

The constant threat of internal rebellions also significantly hampered Kublai Khan's efforts. The sheer size and diversity of the empire made it nearly impossible to quell every uprising swiftly. Furthermore, the Mongol ruling class itself was not immune to internal strife. Succession disputes and power struggles among the elite undermined unity and diverted precious resources away from addressing the more pressing needs of the empire. The constant threat of internal conflict meant that a substantial portion of the military and resources needed to be allocated to maintaining internal stability, leaving less for external defense and expansion.

In conclusion,

managing the vast and diverse Yuan Dynasty presented Kublai Khan with an almost insurmountable set of challenges. The scale of his empire, its cultural heterogeneity, the complexities of integration, economic management, and the constant threat of internal rebellions all contributed to a tumultuous and often unpredictable reign. Kublai Khan's success in maintaining control for as long as he did was a testament to his considerable political acumen, diplomatic skill, and administrative talent, but the inherent difficulties in governing such an immense and diverse empire ultimately proved to be a significant factor in the eventual decline of the Yuan Dynasty.

The Difficulties of Integrating Different Cultures and Ethnicities

Kublai Khan's monumental task of unifying a vast and diverse empire presented unprecedented challenges in integrating disparate cultures and ethnicities. The Yuan Dynasty, born from the conquest of the Song Dynasty and encompassing territories stretching across Eurasia, was a melting pot of Mongols, Chinese, Persians, Arabs, and numerous other groups, each with their own unique traditions, languages, and social structures. This inherent diversity, while contributing to the empire's richness, also became a significant source of tension and instability.

The Mongol elite, accustomed to a nomadic lifestyle and hierarchical social order, often clashed with the sedentary Chinese population, who possessed a sophisticated bureaucracy and a long history of centralized governance. The Mongols, initially relying on their military prowess and a system of direct rule, struggled to effectively administer a complex society like China's. Attempts to impose Mongol customs and laws on the Chinese population met with resistance, exacerbating existing tensions.

One major source of friction stemmed from land ownership and taxation. The Mongols favored a system based on pastoral nomadism, which was drastically different from the established agrarian system of China. Confiscations of land and imposition of new tax structures led to widespread resentment and uprisings among the Chinese peasantry. This created a cycle of rebellion and repression, further undermining the stability of the empire.

Furthermore, cultural misunderstandings and prejudices played a significant role in hindering integration. The Mongols, often viewed as barbarian invaders by the Chinese intellectual elite, struggled to gain their acceptance and cooperation. The Chinese, in turn, were often suspicious of the Mongol's intentions and resistant to cultural assimilation. This mutual distrust further complicated efforts towards a harmonious coexistence.

The Yuan Dynasty's attempts at cultural synthesis were complex and multifaceted. Kublai Khan, recognizing the need for a degree of integration, adopted certain aspects of Chinese culture, including the use of Chinese administrative systems and the patronage of Chinese scholars and artists. However, these efforts were often insufficient to bridge the deep-seated cultural and social divides. The imposition of Mongol practices alongside attempts at cultural accommodation frequently resulted in contradictions and inconsistencies, generating confusion and further unrest.

Religious differences also presented a significant hurdle. While Kublai Khan initially adopted a policy of religious tolerance, accommodating Buddhism, Taoism, Confucianism, Islam, and Christianity, religious tensions occasionally erupted. Disputes over religious practices and the dominance of certain faiths within the empire sometimes led to conflict and social fragmentation.

The challenge of language also played a crucial role. The lack of a common language between the Mongols and the various Chinese populations hampered communication and hindered the effective administration of the empire. While efforts were made to promote the use of certain languages, the linguistic diversity remained a significant barrier to broader cultural integration.

In conclusion, the integration of diverse cultures and ethnicities under the Yuan Dynasty proved to be a formidable challenge for Kublai Khan. Despite attempts at cultural exchange and administrative reforms, deep-seated prejudices, conflicting social structures, and communication barriers consistently hampered the creation of a truly unified and harmonious empire. The lasting legacy of this struggle is evident in the recurrent internal conflicts and ultimately, the relatively short-lived nature of the Yuan Dynasty itself. The story of the Yuan Dynasty serves as a compelling illustration of the immense difficulties inherent in forging unity from such a diverse collection of peoples and cultures, a historical lesson that continues to resonate in the modern world.

Internal Power Struggles and Succession Issues

The vast empire forged by Kublai Khan, a testament to his strategic brilliance and military prowess, was ultimately challenged by the very forces that contributed to its creation: the inherent instability of power dynamics within the Mongol aristocracy and the complex interplay of familial relationships. The question of succession, a recurring theme throughout Mongol history, loomed large during Kublai's later years, threatening to unravel the carefully constructed fabric of the Yuan Dynasty.

Kublai's reign, while characterized by periods of unprecedented prosperity and cultural exchange, was far from serene. The constant struggle for dominance among his numerous sons and relatives created a climate of intrigue and uncertainty. Unlike the relatively clear succession plan established by Genghis Khan, Kublai's attempts to designate an heir proved fraught with difficulty. The lack of a pre-ordained successor invited intense competition, with ambitious princes vying for favor and influence, often resorting to underhanded tactics and outright rebellion.

The absence of a clearly defined system for succession also exacerbated existing tensions within the Mongol court. Different factions, each aligned with a particular prince, emerged, creating a deeply divided court where loyalty was often conditional and based on perceived advantages. This internal fracturing undermined Kublai's authority in his later years and weakened the administrative capabilities of the vast empire.

The complexities of Mongol tribal customs further complicated matters. While Kublai sought to establish a more centralized system of governance based on Chinese models, traditional Mongol practices, particularly regarding inheritance and leadership, continued to influence the power dynamics within the court. This clash between tradition and innovation only amplified the existing tensions, contributing to the atmosphere of uncertainty and rivalry.

One significant aspect of this power struggle was the competition between Kublai's sons. Each prince possessed their own supporters among the Mongol elite, leading to alliances and counter-alliances that frequently shifted depending on the perceived strength and favor of each individual. The lack of a strong consensus on who should succeed Kublai led to intense maneuvering, undermining the stability of the empire and creating opportunities for exploitation by external forces.

The failure to establish a smooth succession not only weakened the Yuan Dynasty during Kublai's final years but also contributed to its eventual decline. The prolonged power struggle that followed Kublai's death resulted in further instability and internal conflict, ultimately paving the way for rebellions and ultimately, the dynasty's collapse. The events surrounding Kublai's death and the ensuing struggle for power serve as a cautionary tale about the fragility of even the most powerful empires when faced with the insidious threat of internal division and the unresolved issue of succession.

The legacy of Kublai Khan's internal struggles is not merely a historical footnote. It serves as a compelling reminder of the *critical importance of well-defined succession plans* in maintaining the stability and longevity of any empire or leadership structure. The intense power plays and uncertainties within his own family demonstrate the *peril of unchecked ambition and the vital need for clear rules of governance* to avoid the chaos and instability that ultimately weakened the Yuan dynasty and hastened its demise.

11. Military Campaigns in Southeast Asia and Japan

The Reasons Behind the Military Expeditions

Kublai Khan's reign, while marked by significant achievements in governance, economic reform, and cultural exchange, was also punctuated by a series of ambitious, yet ultimately uneven, military campaigns. Understanding the motivations behind these expeditions requires examining a complex interplay of factors, ranging from the inherent expansionist tendencies of the Mongol empire to more nuanced considerations of geopolitical strategy, economic gain, and the emperor's personal ambitions.

One primary driver was the ***inherent expansionist impulse*** of the Mongol tradition. Genghis Khan, Kublai's grandfather, had instilled a culture of conquest and territorial expansion, viewing it not simply as a means of accumulating wealth and power, but also as a validation of their divinely ordained right to rule. Kublai, inheriting this legacy, felt compelled to continue the pattern of Mongol dominance, pushing the boundaries of the Yuan Dynasty's influence further afield.

Beyond this inherited ethos, ***strategic geopolitical considerations*** heavily influenced Kublai's military decisions. The Southern Song Dynasty, while weakened, still posed a significant threat to Yuan control over

Southern China. Its subjugation was a strategic imperative for consolidating power and establishing complete dominion over the entire country. Similarly, campaigns in Southeast Asia and beyond aimed to secure vital trade routes and neutralize potential rivals who might challenge Yuan hegemony in the region. The control of maritime trade routes and access to resources in these areas were crucial to maintaining the empire's economic prosperity.

Economic motives played a substantial role. The Mongol Empire relied heavily on tribute and the plunder of conquered territories. Military expeditions offered a means of acquiring vast riches and resources that fueled the Yuan Dynasty's ambitious infrastructure projects and lavish court. Access to spices, precious metals, and other exotic goods from Southeast Asia was particularly alluring, contributing to the economic incentives behind the expeditions into that region. Furthermore, securing trade routes ensured the smooth flow of goods along the Silk Road, bolstering the empire's economy and solidifying its position as a pivotal player in Eurasian commerce.

Finally, *personal ambition and the pursuit of glory* likely contributed to Kublai's decision-making. The emperor, renowned for his intelligence and ambition, might have been driven by a desire to surpass the accomplishments of his ancestors, etching his name in history as one of the greatest conquerors of all time. The conquest of Japan, in particular, appears to have been heavily influenced by Kublai's personal drive to demonstrate his unmatched military power and extend the Yuan Dynasty's reach across the seas, creating a vast maritime empire that would dwarf the existing land-based domains.

In conclusion, the military expeditions undertaken during Kublai Khan's reign were not driven by a single, monolithic motive. Rather, they resulted from a complex interplay of inherited traditions, strategic imperatives, economic incentives, and the emperor's personal ambition. Understanding these multiple factors provides a more nuanced perspective on Kublai Khan's military policies and their impact on the Yuan Dynasty and the broader historical landscape of Eurasia.

It's important to note that while some expeditions, such as the conquest of the Southern Song, were largely successful, others, notably the attempts to conquer Japan, met with disastrous failure, highlighting the inherent limitations and unforeseen challenges that can arise even in the context of seemingly well-planned military campaigns. These failures underscore the complexities of imperial expansion and the unpredictable nature of warfare, reminding us that even the most powerful empires are not immune to setbacks and reversals of fortune.

The Successes and Failures of the Campaigns

Kublai Khan's military ambitions extended beyond the consolidation of power in China. His reign witnessed significant military campaigns, some achieving resounding success, while others ended in ignominious defeat, profoundly shaping the trajectory of the Yuan Dynasty and its place in history. A nuanced examination reveals the complexities of these ventures, highlighting both the strategic brilliance and the inherent limitations of his imperial ambitions.

Among Kublai Khan's most notable military achievements was the **final subjugation of the Southern Song Dynasty**. This protracted conflict, marked by strategic brilliance and relentless perseverance, culminated in the capture of the Song capital and the formal end of a dynasty that had stubbornly resisted Mongol expansion for decades. This victory solidified the Yuan Dynasty's control over all of China, uniting the country under a single rule for the first time in centuries. The integration of formerly independent regions into the vast Mongol empire was a testament to his organizational prowess. This success wasn't merely a military feat but a significant step towards consolidating power and establishing lasting control over a vastly diverse population. The efficiency in integrating conquered territories played a key role in the overall stability of the empire.

However, Kublai Khan's military pursuits were not without their failures. His ambitious attempts to conquer **Japan** in the late 13th century represent a stark contrast to his successes. Two massive naval expeditions, launched with considerable resources and manpower, were utterly destroyed by powerful typhoons, famously known as "kamikaze" or divine winds. These catastrophic defeats not only resulted in the loss of countless soldiers and ships but also significantly depleted the Yuan Dynasty's treasury and military strength. The scale of these losses served as a crucial turning point and a stark reminder of the unpredictable nature of warfare, particularly when confronted by formidable natural forces.

Similarly, his campaigns in **Southeast Asia**, while achieving some initial gains, ultimately proved unsustainable. The vast distances, unfamiliar terrains, and the strong resistance encountered by the Mongol armies ultimately hampered long-term success. The logistical challenges of sustaining a large army so far from its supply lines proved insurmountable. While some territories were temporarily brought under Yuan control, consolidating power in these regions proved both expensive and ultimately unproductive. The costly campaigns drained vital resources that could have been dedicated to domestic affairs and further development. These ultimately failed campaigns demonstrated the limitations of even the most formidable military force when faced with logistical constraints and determined local resistance.

The analysis of Kublai Khan's military campaigns reveals a complex interplay of factors influencing both success and failure. **Strategic planning, logistical efficiency, the adaptability of Mongol military tactics to diverse terrains, and the level of local resistance** all played crucial roles. The successes highlight his military genius and his ability to consolidate power, whereas the failures underscore the limitations of his ambition when confronted with the unpredictable forces of nature and determined adversaries. These campaigns, in their totality, formed an essential chapter in the history of the Yuan Dynasty, shaping its internal dynamics, its economic resources, and its overall geopolitical standing.

The legacy of these campaigns is not merely one of military victories and defeats, but a more nuanced understanding of Kublai Khan's reign, showcasing his strategic capabilities, his administrative weaknesses, and the complex challenges involved in managing a vast and diverse empire.

The impact of these campaigns on the empire's resources and reputation

Kublai Khan's military expeditions into Southeast Asia and Japan, while ambitious in scope, significantly impacted the Yuan Dynasty's resources and its international reputation, leaving a complex and multifaceted legacy.

The campaigns in Southeast Asia, primarily targeting the kingdoms of Champa and Annam (modern-day Vietnam), initially yielded some success. **The acquisition of Champa's coastal regions provided access to valuable trade routes and resources**. However, these gains came at a steep price. Prolonged warfare drained the Yuan treasury, diverting resources from crucial internal projects like infrastructure development and agricultural improvements. The constant need to replenish troops and supplies stretched the empire's logistical capabilities to their limits, hindering economic growth and stability within the heartland.

The **Japanese expeditions**, famously known as the Mongol invasions of Japan (1274 and 1281), proved far more disastrous. These ambitious attempts to conquer the islands met with fierce resistance from the samurai and were ultimately thwarted by **typhoons**, which became legendary in Japanese folklore as "kamikaze" (divine winds). The financial and human costs were staggering. The massive fleets, meticulously assembled and equipped, were largely destroyed. **Thousands of soldiers perished**, representing a substantial loss of military manpower and expertise. The failure further damaged the Yuan Dynasty's prestige and military reputation, weakening its standing in East Asia.

Beyond the direct material costs, *the impact on the Yuan Dynasty's reputation was profound*. The failure of the Japanese invasions, in particular, shattered the image of invincibility that the Mongol Empire had previously cultivated. **News of the setbacks spread quickly, undermining the Yuan's authority and credibility among both its subjects and neighboring states**. This loss of prestige contributed to the rise of internal dissent and rebellion, making it increasingly difficult to maintain control over the vast and diverse empire. The perception of the Yuan as a less powerful force emboldened rivals and potential adversaries, creating new challenges to its dominance.

The cumulative effect of these campaigns was a significant drain on the empire's resources, both human and financial. The considerable investments in these military ventures yielded minimal long-term benefits, while the failures inflicted considerable damage to the Yuan's military standing and overall reputation, ultimately contributing to its internal vulnerabilities and eventual decline.

While the Southeast Asian conquests brought some temporary territorial gains and access to trade routes, **the costly nature of these campaigns and the strategic setbacks in Japan ultimately outweighed any potential advantages**. These military endeavors left a lasting legacy – a weakened treasury, a depleted military, and a tarnished international reputation that profoundly affected the stability and longevity of Kublai Khan's empire.

Analysis of Military Strategies and Their Effectiveness

Kublai Khan's military campaigns, a defining aspect of his reign, reveal a complex interplay of innovative strategies, logistical prowess, and the inherent limitations of imperial expansion. While his conquests initially showcased remarkable tactical acumen, the later years highlighted the challenges of sustaining dominance over vast and diverse territories.

His early successes against the Southern Song Dynasty, culminating in the fall of Xiangyang in 1273, exemplify his masterful adaptation of Mongol warfare to siege operations. Unlike the swift, devastating cavalry charges characteristic of earlier Mongol conquests, the prolonged siege of Xiangyang required a sustained commitment of resources and a sophisticated understanding of siege weaponry and tactics. This demonstrated **Kublai Khan's willingness to evolve his military doctrine** to overcome challenges posed by fortified cities and technologically advanced opponents. He effectively combined traditional Mongol horsemanship with the latest innovations in siege technology, effectively leveraging both brute force and strategic planning.

The *integration of Chinese siege engineers and naval expertise* into his military further underscores his pragmatic approach. This collaboration not only enhanced his military capabilities but also facilitated the incorporation of conquered territories into the expanding Yuan Dynasty. The adoption of advanced shipbuilding techniques allowed for successful naval campaigns and the establishment of maritime control, enabling the supply and movement of his armies along extended coastlines and waterways.

However, Kublai Khan's later military ventures proved less successful. His ambitious expeditions against Japan (1274 and 1281) and Southeast Asia, while showcasing his ambition to further extend the empire's reach, ultimately highlight the limitations of his logistical capabilities when operating far from his core territories. These campaigns were hampered by severe typhoons, known as "kamikaze", undermining the effectiveness of his considerable naval might and demonstrating the **impact of unforeseen circumstances** on even the most well-planned military operations. The sheer scale of these expeditions, coupled with the logistical complexities of supplying armies across vast distances, stretched the resources of the Yuan Dynasty to their limits.

Furthermore, the *resistance encountered in these campaigns* underscores the inherent difficulties of imposing Mongol rule on populations with strong cultural and national identities. While military might could secure initial victories, establishing lasting control demanded a different approach, emphasizing diplomacy and political accommodation rather than solely relying on military dominance. The subsequent decline of the Yuan Dynasty demonstrates that military power alone is insufficient for the lasting establishment of a stable and prosperous empire. A complex interplay of military prowess, adaptable strategy, economic and logistical efficiency, and sound political acumen is essential for sustained imperial success. Kublai Khan's reign provides a compelling case study for examining this intricate interplay of factors influencing both the successes and eventual limitations of imperial ambitions.

The analysis of Kublai Khan's military strategies reveals a pattern of initial success rooted in adaptation, innovation, and efficient logistical support, followed by a period where ambitious expansion strained resources and highlighted the limitations of imposing rule solely through force. His campaigns serve as a critical examination of the complex relationship between military might, political strategy, and the sustainable management of an expansive empire. The effectiveness of his military strategies, while significant in his early conquests, ultimately reveals the need for a more holistic approach to imperial governance for long-term stability.

12. The Later Years of Kublai Khan: Reflections on Reign

The aging emperor's policies and decisions in his later years

As the weight of years settled upon Kublai Khan, a perceptible shift occurred in his governance, a transformation reflecting both the physical toll of age and the accumulating complexities of his vast empire. His once-iron grip on power, though still formidable, showed signs of loosening, leading to significant changes in policy and decision-making.

One of the most notable alterations in Kublai Khan's later years was a discernible decline in his aggressive expansionist policies. The ambitious campaigns that had defined much of his earlier reign, such as the ill-fated invasions of Japan and Southeast Asia, gradually gave way to a more cautious, introspective approach. **The sheer cost and strain of maintaining control over such a sprawling empire**, coupled with the mounting internal pressures, likely contributed to this shift. Instead of pursuing further territorial conquests, Kublai Khan increasingly focused on consolidating his existing power and addressing the growing internal instability within the Yuan Dynasty.

This change in approach manifested in his domestic policies. While his earlier years were marked by ambitious infrastructure projects and economic reforms, the later years saw a gradual slowdown in such large-scale initiatives. **The focus shifted from grand visions of expansion to more immediate concerns of administrative efficiency and stability.** This involved streamlining bureaucratic processes, addressing corruption within the government, and attempting to alleviate the burdens faced by the populace. Evidence suggests an effort to improve the livelihoods of ordinary citizens, perhaps as a means to strengthen his support base and curb growing discontent.

However, the aging emperor's capacity for decisive action was demonstrably hampered by both physical and mental fatigue. While he retained his keen intellect, his ability to oversee the intricate web of affairs across his empire was diminished. This led to a greater reliance on his advisors and family members, resulting in some instances of flawed decision-making. The increasing influence of court factions and internal power struggles further complicated his governance, often leading to indecisive policies or actions that ultimately proved detrimental to the empire's stability.

Succession became a paramount concern in Kublai Khan's twilight years. The question of who would inherit the vast Yuan Empire weighed heavily on his mind, leading to significant shifts in court dynamics and the rise of rival claimants. This period was marked by intense political maneuvering and jockeying for power among members of the royal family. While Kublai Khan attempted to secure a smooth succession, his efforts were partially undermined by internal strife and the unresolved tensions between competing factions within the empire.

In his final years, Kublai Khan's actions suggest a profound reflection on his life and legacy. *While still committed to maintaining order and stability within his realm*, the scale of his ambitions diminished. He seemed to recognize the inherent limitations of imperial power, the challenges of governing such a diverse population, and the inevitability of decline. His legacy, once defined by ambitious expansion, began to be re-evaluated in the context of long-term governance and cultural integration. **Though his later years were marked by a degree of weariness and compromise**, they nevertheless reveal a ruler attempting to reconcile his grand vision with the realities of age and the inherent fragilities of his empire. The twilight of his reign provides crucial insights into the challenges of maintaining power, fostering unity within a diverse population and the profound reflections that can come with aging and the burden of leadership.

Changes in his Governing Style and Approach

As Kublai Khan aged, a perceptible shift occurred in his governing style and approach, reflecting the cumulative weight of decades spent ruling a vast and diverse empire. This evolution wasn't a sudden transformation, but rather a gradual adjustment shaped by both personal experience and the evolving challenges of his reign.

In his earlier years, Kublai's leadership was characterized by **aggressive expansionism** and a **relentless pursuit of military victories**. His campaigns, while often successful, demanded significant resources and exacted a toll on both the empire's manpower and its treasury. This approach, while effective in consolidating power and expanding the Yuan Dynasty's reach, also sowed the seeds of future instability. The relentless pressure of military campaigns and the strain of managing conquered territories placed immense burdens on the administration and the populace.

As the years wore on, a marked *shift towards consolidation and internal reform* became evident. The ambitious military projects of his youth gradually gave way to a more **introspective approach** focusing on the internal stability and economic well-being of his empire. This change wasn't solely a response to age and waning physical strength; it was driven by hard-earned lessons derived from the challenges of managing such a complex and diverse realm.

One crucial aspect of this change was his **growing reliance on experienced Chinese advisors**. While initially favoring Mongol officials and maintaining a distinct Mongol elite, Kublai increasingly recognized the value of incorporating the skills and knowledge of the Chinese bureaucratic class. This marked a strategic shift, demonstrating a greater appreciation for the existing administrative structures and expertise within the Chinese population. This was not simply about practicality; it represented a gradual acceptance of a more integrated approach to governance, acknowledging the limits of relying solely on a foreign elite to manage a predominantly Chinese population.

Further illustrating this change was his **increased focus on economic development**. The emphasis shifted from purely military conquests towards infrastructural improvements, economic reforms, and the promotion of trade along the Silk Road. Grandiose building projects, such as the expansion of Khanbaliq (modern-day Beijing), were undertaken not merely as expressions of imperial power but also as engines of economic growth and cultural exchange. This reflected a long-term vision extending beyond immediate military gains, highlighting a focus on sustained prosperity and stability.

However, this **transition wasn't without its challenges**. Kublai faced resistance from within his own court, where some Mongol nobles clung to traditional values and resisted the growing influence of Chinese officials. Navigating these internal power struggles became increasingly complex as he aged, requiring deft diplomacy and political acumen. Moreover, the empire's vastness and diverse populations continued to pose significant administrative hurdles, making effective governance a constant struggle.

In his later years, his decision-making process might have become more *deliberative and cautious*, reflecting a growing awareness of the limitations of imperial power and the inherent fragility of such a vast empire. He likely faced increased introspection and perhaps even regret over past decisions, especially concerning the unsuccessful Japanese expedition. The weight of responsibility, combined with the realities of aging, seemingly led to a different, perhaps more nuanced, approach to leadership, characterized by a focus on stability and long-term planning over immediate military expansion.

Ultimately, the changes in Kublai Khan's governing style represent a complex and fascinating evolution. His journey reflects not only the demands of governing a sprawling empire, but also the personal growth and adaptation of a remarkable historical figure grappling with the legacy of his conquests and the challenge of building a lasting dynasty.

His Reflections on Life and Achievements

As Kublai Khan approached the twilight of his long and impactful reign, the weight of years and the vastness of his accomplishments undoubtedly pressed upon his mind. What were his thoughts as he looked back upon a life that had reshaped the political and cultural landscape of Eurasia? What reflections did this extraordinary man harbor, and how did he assess the legacy he would leave behind?

Historians can only speculate, piecing together clues from the scant personal accounts and the monumental scale of his rule. Yet, it seems plausible to surmise that Kublai, despite his unwavering ambition, was not immune to introspection. The sheer scope of his endeavors – the unification of disparate Mongol tribes, the conquest and integration of China, the ambitious expansion of trade along the Silk Road, and the patronage of diverse cultures – must have been staggering. The successes, and undoubtedly the failures, of these grand designs would have certainly been subjects of intense contemplation.

His early life, marked by the shadow of his illustrious grandfather, Genghis Khan, must have presented both inspiration and immense pressure. The **burden of expectation** to match, or even surpass, Genghis's achievements must have been considerable. Did he ever feel the weight of his inheritance, the constant comparison with the founder of the Mongol Empire? Did he feel a sense of fulfillment in having carved his own path to power, in forging his own unique identity as the founder of the Yuan Dynasty?

The integration of conquered territories and peoples was a constant challenge throughout Kublai's reign. While he initially promoted tolerance and cultural exchange, the **tensions between the Mongol elite and the Chinese population** never truly disappeared. He witnessed rebellions and uprisings that tested the limits of his power and forced him to confront the *complexities of empire building*. Did he, in his later years, reflect on the <u>successes and failures</u> of his policies, on his attempts to bridge the cultural divides and forge a unified empire? Did he consider whether a more forceful approach or a gentler hand would have yielded different results?

The failed Japanese invasions, another significant episode in his reign, likely provided ample opportunity for self-reflection. The scale of the undertaking, and the catastrophic loss of men and resources, would have been difficult to ignore. Did he question his judgment, analyze the factors that led to the devastating defeats, and ponder on the risks of overextension in his quest for global dominance? Or did he choose to view it as simply another chapter in the ongoing saga of his grand imperial design?

His interactions with figures like Marco Polo, a fascinating emissary from the far West, would have provided another dimension to his introspection. The accounts of the Venetian traveler offered Kublai a glimpse of a world vastly different from his own, **potentially sparking thoughts about the interconnectedness of human societies** and the significance of cultural exchange. Did he see his empire as a pivotal link in a larger global network, or did he primarily focus on its internal strength and stability?

Finally, the question of legacy must have occupied a prominent place in Kublai's reflections. Did he hope that his name would be etched in history as a builder of empires, a patron of arts and learning, a shrewd diplomat, a skilled military commander? Or did he grapple with the realization that even the mightiest empires are ultimately transient, subject to the inexorable march of time? *His personal assessment of his life's work, alas, remains lost to us, hidden behind the veil of history.* Yet, his actions, his decisions, and his grand vision continue to inspire debate and provide a captivating glimpse into the complexities of ruling an empire that spanned continents and cultures.

Preparing for succession and the future of the Yuan Dynasty

*The twilight of Kublai Khan's reign was not simply a matter of physical decline; it was a period marked by profound anxieties regarding the future of the Yuan Dynasty, a vast and complex empire he had painstakingly constructed. The **question of succession** loomed large, casting a long shadow over the final years of his life. Unlike the relatively straightforward succession processes seen in some dynasties, Kublai's path to power had been fraught with internal struggles and political maneuvering. This experience colored his approach to appointing an heir, a decision laden with significant implications for the stability and longevity of the Yuan Empire.*

The emperor's advanced age and the inherent instability associated with dynastic transitions created a climate of uncertainty. His **health deteriorated** noticeably, making his ability to actively manage affairs increasingly precarious. This vulnerability did not escape the sharp eyes of the Mongol elite, who engaged in subtle but intense power struggles, vying for favor and influence. The

absence of a clear, universally accepted successor fuelled speculation and potentially destabilizing alliances. Each faction sought to advance the prospects of their preferred candidate, creating a complicated web of loyalties and betrayals.

Kublai, aware of these undercurrents, attempted to navigate the treacherous political landscape. He sought to **groom a suitable successor**, a process complicated by the complexities of Mongol customs and the delicate balance required to maintain unity within the diverse population of his empire. The <u>choice was not merely a matter of lineage</u>; it also depended on the candidate's demonstrated administrative abilities, military prowess, and diplomatic skills. Moreover, the selected heir needed to maintain the equilibrium between the Mongol aristocracy and the Chinese bureaucracy, a delicate balancing act critical to the empire's survival.

The **economic and administrative stability** of the Yuan Dynasty was inextricably linked to the succession process. Any abrupt or contested transfer of power risked triggering unrest, potentially leading to revolts or internal conflicts that could fragment the empire. Kublai understood that the smooth transition of power was vital to maintaining the economic prosperity and administrative effectiveness he had established. This involved not just the appointment of a new ruler but also the careful management of the transition period, a time fraught with uncertainty.

Kublai's *efforts to prepare for succession* extended beyond merely appointing an heir. He likely engaged in extensive consultations with trusted advisors, weighing their insights and gauging their loyalty. He might have implemented measures aimed at strengthening the bureaucratic structures, ensuring a consistent flow of governance even amidst the transition. This would have included reinforcing the existing administrative framework and ensuring loyalty among key officials, which could mitigate any power vacuum.

However, despite his careful planning, the **inherent challenges of succession** proved insurmountable. His chosen heir, ultimately, proved inadequate to the task. The resulting instability and conflicts in the wake of his death signaled the fragility of the empire he built, revealing the limitations even of a ruler as powerful and influential as Kublai Khan. *The seeds of the Yuan Dynasty's eventual decline* were sown in this turbulent period of transition, reminding us that even the most carefully constructed empires are vulnerable to the pressures of succession and internal strife.

The story of Kublai Khan's preparations for succession thus highlights a crucial paradox of imperial power: the ability to build and maintain a vast empire often clashed with the enduring challenges of securing its future through peaceful succession. It serves as a cautionary tale, revealing the complexities of imperial legacy and the precarious nature of even the most formidable empires. Kublai's final years offer a compelling study of how even the most astute rulers grapple with the enduring problems of power, transition, and the ultimate limitations of imperial authority.

Part V: The Enduring Impact

13. The Death of Kublai Khan: The End of an Era

Kublai Khan's Death and the Transition of Power

The year 1294 marked a pivotal moment in the history of the Yuan Dynasty and, indeed, East Asia. The death of Kublai Khan, after a long and impactful reign, ushered in an era of uncertainty and shifting power dynamics. His passing was not merely the end of a life; it was the end of an epoch, leaving behind a legacy both profound and complex.

Kublai Khan's demise, though anticipated given his advanced age, was not without its drama. Accounts from the period, while often fragmented and colored by the perspectives of different factions, paint a picture of intrigue and jockeying for position amongst the emperor's family and court officials. The absence of a clear and undisputed successor, despite Kublai's efforts to establish a line of inheritance, immediately plunged the Yuan court into a maelstrom of political maneuvering.

Unlike his grandfather, Genghis Khan, who had consolidated his authority through decisive military actions and the unwavering loyalty of his generals, Kublai Khan had ruled a vast and diverse empire characterized by intricate political relationships between Mongol elites and the Chinese bureaucracy. This intricacy, while fostering economic and cultural growth during his reign, complicated the succession process significantly. The absence of a strong military figure capable of imposing his will immediately created power vacuums, leading to intense competition for control.

The immediate period following Kublai Khan's death was marked by a fierce struggle for power among his grandsons. While Temür, Kublai's eldest surviving son, held a prominent position, his claim to the throne was contested. The ensuing power struggle revealed deep divisions within the Mongol elite, highlighting the limitations of Kublai's attempts to integrate Mongol and Chinese traditions and institutions. The interplay between Mongol military strength and the sophisticated Chinese administrative structures, a feature of Kublai's reign, contributed to the complexity of the succession crisis.

The transition of power was not a smooth or swift affair. It involved a series of intrigues, alliances, and betrayals, with various factions vying for control. The eventual ascendance of one successor over others was not simply a matter of birthright or military might but rather the result of intricate political machinations, demonstrating the intricacies of power in a vast, multi-cultural empire. The fragility of the power structures established by Kublai became painfully apparent.

The period of succession ultimately contributed to instability that would eventually weaken the Yuan Dynasty, and pave the way for its eventual decline. This period of transition, marked by political fragmentation and internal strife, severely hampered the empire's ability to deal with external threats and internal rebellions. The subsequent emperors struggled to maintain the vast territory and the cohesive power structure established during Kublai's reign.

In conclusion, Kublai Khan's death was not just a personal event; it served as a critical turning point in the Yuan Dynasty's history. The chaotic succession and the subsequent internal power struggles revealed the inherent vulnerabilities of a multi-ethnic empire built on the foundation of both military conquest and political negotiation. The lack of a clear and widely accepted heir, combined with the inherent tensions between Mongol and Chinese elites, had far-reaching consequences that foreshadowed the eventual decline and fall of the Yuan dynasty decades later. The legacy of this period serves as a stark reminder of the delicate balance required to sustain a multi-cultural empire.

Reactions to his death within the empire and abroad

The passing of Kublai Khan in 1294 CE marked not merely the end of a life, but a pivotal turning point in the trajectory of the Yuan Dynasty and the broader Eurasian landscape. His death reverberated across vast distances, triggering a cascade of reactions that varied widely in intensity and character, depending on the perspectives and vested interests of those affected.

Within the vast empire itself, the immediate response was one of uncertainty and apprehension. The complex succession dynamics, long a simmering concern during

Kublai's later years, now exploded into the open. His designated successor, Temür, faced immediate challenges to his authority from various factions within the Mongol aristocracy, each vying for influence and control over the sprawling realm. The rumors and power struggles that followed Kublai's death plunged the court into a period of instability, threatening the carefully constructed political order he had maintained.

The Chinese populace, long subjected to Mongol rule, reacted with a mix of emotions. While some may have harbored hopes for improved governance or a potential weakening of Mongol authority, others likely viewed the change of leadership with trepidation, uncertain of what the future held under a new emperor. The legacy of Kublai's reign, which involved both periods of relative prosperity and significant hardship, would undoubtedly shape interpretations of his death and expectations for his successor.

Beyond the borders of the Yuan Dynasty, the news of Kublai's death traveled along the well-established trade routes and diplomatic channels of the era. Neighboring states, some of whom had been allies, and others rivals, closely monitored the events unfolding in the Yuan court. Potential rivals likely saw the emperor's death as an opportunity to challenge the Yuan's dominance, while long-standing allies may have worried about the implications for their own security and the stability of regional trade relations. The shift in leadership created a significant vacuum in the political and economic landscape of Eurasia.

In the West, the news may have been greeted with a mixture of curiosity and speculation. While accounts of Kublai Khan's reign had filtered through to Europe via travelers like Marco Polo, the true scale of his empire and its internal dynamics remained largely mysterious. The death of such a powerful ruler undoubtedly triggered renewed discussions and assessments of the Mongol Empire's strength and future prospects. News of the succession crisis might have been interpreted in various ways, ranging from concerns over the stability of trade routes to opportunities for renewed Western expansion.

Ultimately, Kublai Khan's death served as a watershed moment. It exposed the inherent fragilities of the Yuan Dynasty, despite its vast size and apparent strength. The ensuing power struggles and succession crises foreshadowed the eventual decline of the dynasty, but also highlighted the lasting impact of his rule on the political, economic, and cultural landscape of Eurasia. His passing triggered a chain reaction across continents, affecting not only the internal workings of his empire but also shaping the perceptions and policies of neighboring states and distant powers, underscoring the far-reaching influence of his remarkable reign.

The responses to Kublai Khan's death, therefore, were diverse and multifaceted, reflecting the complexities of his reign and the diverse actors involved within and beyond the boundaries of the Yuan Dynasty. It was not just the end of an era, but the beginning of a new and uncertain chapter in the history of East Asia and beyond.

The Legacy He Left Behind for Future Generations

Kublai Khan's death in 1294 marked the end of an era, but his impact resonated far beyond his lifetime, shaping the course of history in profound and multifaceted ways. His legacy is a complex tapestry woven from threads of military conquest, political innovation, economic reform, and cultural exchange.

His most immediate legacy was the **Yuan Dynasty**, a powerful empire that unified much of China under Mongol rule for nearly a century. While the dynasty eventually fell, its establishment profoundly altered the political and social landscape of China. The Yuan period witnessed the introduction of new administrative systems, legal codes, and economic policies, many of which influenced subsequent Chinese dynasties. The **integration of Mongol and Chinese cultures**, though often fraught with tension, led to a unique cultural synthesis, enriching both sides. This period of exchange saw advancements in art, literature, and technology, leaving an indelible mark on Chinese culture.

Beyond China's borders, Kublai Khan's legacy extended through his **expansion of the Silk Road**. His reign saw a flourishing of trade and cultural exchange across Eurasia, connecting distant civilizations and facilitating the flow of goods, ideas, and technologies. The increased connectivity fostered by his policies contributed to a period of economic prosperity and cultural diffusion, influencing societies from the Middle East to Europe. The tales of Marco Polo, a testament to this increased connectivity, helped shape European perceptions of the East, inspiring future exploration and trade.

His emphasis on **religious tolerance** stands out as a significant aspect of his legacy. Unlike many rulers of his time, Kublai Khan fostered a degree of religious pluralism, allowing Buddhism, Taoism, Confucianism, Islam, and Christianity to coexist within his empire. While this tolerance wasn't absolute, it fostered a climate of relative peace and allowed for a richer cultural exchange. This policy stands in contrast to many historical instances of religious persecution and demonstrates a relatively open-minded approach to governance.

However, Kublai Khan's legacy is not without its shadows. His military campaigns, while expanding the empire, also resulted in significant loss of life and destruction. The failed attempts to conquer Japan and the subjugation of various peoples throughout his reign demonstrate the brutality inherent in imperial expansion. While his reign brought periods of prosperity, it also saw periods of instability, rebellion, and internal conflict, revealing the challenges of ruling such a vast and diverse empire.

In conclusion, Kublai Khan's legacy is one of **contradictions and complexities**. He was a ruthless conqueror, a brilliant strategist, a patron of the arts, and a promoter of trade. His reign shaped the course of history in China, across Asia, and even in Europe. His impact is visible in the cultural exchange that flourished under his rule, the economic innovations that propelled his empire, and the lasting effects of the Yuan Dynasty's policies on Chinese society. Understanding Kublai Khan's legacy requires acknowledging both the achievements and the failings of his reign, presenting a complete and nuanced understanding of a pivotal figure in world history.

The Subsequent Decline of the Yuan Dynasty

The death of Kublai Khan in 1294 marked not an end, but a turning point. While his reign had witnessed unparalleled expansion and cultural synthesis, the seeds of the Yuan Dynasty's decline were already sown.

The immediate aftermath saw a power struggle amongst Kublai's heirs, a familiar theme within the Mongol Empire. The lack of a clear and strong successor, coupled with the inherent instability of a vast multi-ethnic empire, created fertile ground for dissent. Succession crises weakened the central authority, empowering regional potentates and fostering internal strife. The efficient centralized administration established by Kublai began to crumble under the weight of internal conflicts and weakening leadership.

Economic woes further exacerbated the dynasty's fragility. The ambitious infrastructure projects and generous patronage of the arts, while enriching the Yuan culture, also placed a significant strain on the imperial treasury. Overspending and inefficient tax collection systems contributed to economic instability. This financial vulnerability made the Yuan Empire increasingly susceptible to internal rebellions and external threats. The vast distances and logistical challenges inherent in governing such a sprawling empire made it increasingly difficult to maintain control over peripheral regions.

The growing resentment amongst the Chinese populace, fueled by decades of Mongol rule, provided the impetus for widespread rebellions. While Kublai had attempted a degree of cultural integration, many Chinese felt alienated by Mongol customs and policies. The imposition of Mongol administrators and the preferential treatment afforded to Mongol elites fueled this resentment. The later Yuan emperors, lacking Kublai's political acumen and administrative skills, failed to address these underlying tensions, allowing them to fester and eventually erupt into open revolt.

The Red Turban Rebellion, beginning in the early 14th century, proved to be a decisive turning point. This large-scale uprising, rooted in religious fervor and fueled by social and economic inequalities, challenged the Yuan's authority on a scale unlike any seen before. The rebellion's success was not solely attributable to its size, but also to the Yuan Dynasty's internal weaknesses. The empire's military strength, once a cornerstone of its power, had been depleted by years of internal conflicts and economic hardship, leaving it vulnerable to the sustained onslaught of the rebels.

The military's inability to quell the rebellion effectively hastened the Yuan Dynasty's collapse. The Mongols' traditional military prowess, honed on the steppes, proved less effective against the guerilla warfare tactics employed by the rebels. The loss of key battles and the gradual erosion of territorial control demonstrated the Yuan's waning military capability and the ultimate failure of its governing system.

By the 1360s, the Yuan Dynasty was on the brink of collapse. The final blow came with the emergence of Zhu Yuanzhang, a former Buddhist monk, who rose through the ranks of the rebel army to become the founder of the Ming Dynasty. *Zhu Yuanzhang's forces decisively defeated the Yuan army*, culminating in the capture of Dadu (modern-day Beijing) in 1368. The remaining Mongol forces retreated north, marking the official end of the Yuan Dynasty in China and initiating a new era in Chinese history. The once-mighty empire, built on the foundations of conquest and ambition, ultimately succumbed to internal strife, economic instability, and the rising power of its adversaries.

The decline of the Yuan Dynasty serves as a potent reminder of the fragility of even the most powerful empires, illustrating how internal divisions and economic mismanagement can ultimately lead to their downfall.

14. The Yuan Dynasty's Contribution to Chinese History

The Lasting Impact of the Yuan Dynasty on China's Political, Economic, and Cultural Landscape.

The Yuan Dynasty, established by Kublai Khan in 1271, represents a pivotal, albeit often overlooked, chapter in Chinese history. Its impact reverberated across the political, economic, and cultural spheres, leaving a legacy that continues to shape modern China. While often characterized by its foreign origins, a closer examination reveals a far more nuanced story of interaction, adaptation, and enduring transformation.

Politically, the Yuan Dynasty introduced a novel administrative system that blended Mongol traditions with existing Chinese practices. The **centralized** structure, with its emphasis on direct imperial control, differed significantly from the preceding Song Dynasty's more decentralized approach. While this centralization fostered greater **administrative efficiency** in some aspects, it also led to challenges in governance, particularly in managing a vast and diverse empire. The **implementation of a new legal code**, which aimed to unify disparate legal systems, further highlights the Dynasty's attempt to establish a unified political identity. However, this process of unification wasn't without its complexities and contradictions, leading to both cooperation and conflict between Mongol rulers and the Chinese bureaucracy. The impact of the centralized governance system would linger long after the Yuan's demise, influencing subsequent dynasties and the overall development of Chinese state structure.

Economically, the Yuan Dynasty witnessed a period of significant expansion and change. The **revival of the Silk Road** under Mongol rule led to increased trade and economic prosperity, connecting East and West in unprecedented ways. **International trade** flourished, resulting in increased revenue for the Yuan government, but also leading to the influx of foreign goods and ideas. This economic boom was further fueled by **infrastructure projects** undertaken during Kublai Khan's reign, such as the construction of canals and roads, which facilitated trade and enhanced communication throughout the empire. The Yuan government also played an active role in **monetary policy**, issuing paper currency and implementing various financial reforms, with both positive and negative consequences for the economy. While this era brought significant wealth to certain sectors, it also introduced new economic challenges, including inflation and uneven distribution of wealth across the diverse populations. The lasting economic impact of the Yuan was the establishment of a more interconnected and internationalized economy and a foundation for the development of future trade networks in China.

Culturally, the Yuan Dynasty was a period of remarkable **cultural exchange and synthesis**. The Mongol court was notably cosmopolitan, embracing various cultural traditions. The **religious tolerance** of Kublai Khan allowed for the coexistence of Buddhism, Taoism, Confucianism, Islam, and Christianity, fostering a unique environment of intellectual and artistic interaction. While the Mongols initially exerted significant influence over Chinese culture, the interaction between the two cultures wasn't a one-way street; rather, there was significant cultural exchange and adaptation. Mongol artistic styles blended with existing Chinese traditions, resulting in hybrid forms of art and architecture. The influx of foreign ideas and technologies also contributed to the dynamic evolution of Chinese culture. The Yuan Dynasty's legacy in this area lies not simply in the dominance of one culture over another, but in the lasting intermingling of diverse traditions. The traces of Yuan-era artistic innovation, intellectual ferment, and religious syncretism remain visible in various aspects of contemporary Chinese culture.

In conclusion,

the Yuan Dynasty's impact on China was multifaceted and profound. While its foreign origins initially created significant challenges, the era also marked a period of significant political reorganization, economic expansion, and cultural exchange. The dynasty's legacy is not simply one of conquest and rule but a more complex narrative of interaction, adaptation, and lasting transformation, which continues to shape China's political, economic, and cultural landscape to this day. The seeds of modernization, the development of centralized governance, and the integration of East and West were sown during this period, highlighting the lasting impact and nuanced complexity of the Yuan Dynasty.

The Integration of Mongol and Chinese Cultures

*The reign of Kublai Khan marked a pivotal moment in history, not merely for the establishment of the Yuan Dynasty, but for the unprecedented **cultural synthesis** between the nomadic Mongols and the sophisticated Chinese civilization. This integration, far from being a simple imposition of one culture upon another, was a complex and dynamic process, shaped by political pragmatism, economic necessity, and the surprising adaptability of both cultures.*

Initially, the Mongol conquest was viewed with trepidation by the Chinese populace. The Mongols, with their distinct customs, language, and nomadic lifestyle, were perceived as foreign invaders. However, Kublai Khan, unlike some of his predecessors, recognized the **strategic value** of integrating the Chinese into his administration and society. This was not a mere act of benevolence; it was a pragmatic decision vital for the stability and prosperity of his vast empire. The Chinese bureaucracy, with its centuries-old tradition of administrative efficiency, proved essential for governing such a sprawling territory.

One of the key aspects of this integration was the **adoption of Chinese administrative structures** and practices. While retaining some aspects of the Mongol military organization, Kublai Khan increasingly relied on the existing Chinese governmental framework. Chinese officials were appointed to high positions, and the intricate systems of taxation, record-keeping, and law enforcement were largely maintained. This move not only ensured efficient governance but also demonstrated a willingness to learn from and incorporate the strengths of the conquered civilization.

Beyond the political realm, the integration extended to **economic policies**. Kublai Khan understood the importance of promoting trade and economic prosperity for his empire. He actively encouraged trade along the Silk Road, leading to an unprecedented flourishing of commerce and exchange of goods and ideas. This economic synergy facilitated cultural interaction, bringing together merchants, artisans, and scholars from different parts of the empire. Chinese innovations in technology, agriculture, and manufacturing were adopted and adapted by the Mongols, while Mongol expertise in animal husbandry and military techniques influenced Chinese society.

The cultural exchange also manifested in the realm of **religion and art**. While the Mongols themselves were primarily followers of shamanistic traditions, Kublai Khan adopted a policy of religious tolerance. Buddhism, Confucianism, Taoism, Islam, and Christianity all found a place in the Yuan court. This religious pluralism fostered an environment of intellectual exchange and cross-cultural fertilization. The architecture of the capital, Khanbaliq (present-day Beijing), reflected this blending of cultural influences, showcasing the synthesis of Mongol and Chinese architectural styles.

However, the integration was not without its **challenges**. Social divisions persisted, with tensions between the Mongol ruling class and the Chinese population remaining a recurring theme. The dominance of the Mongol elite in military and political power often created resentment and resistance among the Chinese. Furthermore, the imposition of certain Mongol customs and laws sometimes clashed with established Chinese traditions and caused friction.

Despite these tensions, the cultural exchange between the Mongols and the Chinese under Kublai Khan resulted in a period of significant artistic and intellectual flourishing. New artistic styles emerged, reflecting the fusion of Mongol and Chinese artistic sensibilities. Literary works and philosophical discussions often engaged with themes of cross-cultural understanding and adaptation. This rich tapestry of cultural interaction left an enduring legacy on the art, literature, and intellectual landscape of China.

In conclusion, the integration of Mongol and Chinese cultures under Kublai Khan was a multifaceted and complex process, marked by both cooperation and conflict. While the Mongol conquest initially involved dominance and disruption, Kublai Khan's pragmatic policies fostered a significant degree of cultural synthesis, resulting in a vibrant era of cross-cultural exchange that profoundly shaped the history of both civilizations. The Yuan Dynasty stands as a testament to the possibility of constructive interaction between seemingly disparate cultures, leaving a legacy that continues to fascinate and inspire historians and scholars today.

The Long-Term Effects of Yuan Policies on Chinese Society

Kublai Khan's reign, while undeniably a transformative period in Chinese history, left a complex and multifaceted legacy on Chinese society, the effects of which resonated for centuries. His policies, a blend of Mongol pragmatism and adaptation to Chinese administrative structures, produced both positive and negative consequences that continue to shape scholarly debate.

One of the most significant long-term impacts was the **economic restructuring**. While the initial Mongol conquests disrupted traditional economic systems, the Yuan Dynasty eventually implemented policies designed to stimulate trade and economic growth. The **revival of the Silk Road** under Kublai Khan, coupled with the introduction of paper money and the standardization of weights and measures, fostered economic integration across Eurasia. However, this prosperity was not evenly distributed. Many Chinese merchants prospered, but the reliance on foreign trade and the neglect of agriculture in some regions led to *periodic economic instability* and heightened vulnerability to external shocks.

The Yuan Dynasty's administrative reforms also had lasting effects. The integration of Mongol and Chinese administrative practices created a unique bureaucratic system. While initially dominated by Mongol officials, the Yuan administration increasingly incorporated Chinese scholars and administrators. This gradual **Sinicization of the Yuan bureaucracy** paved the way for the eventual return to a more traditional Chinese-led administration. However, the legacy of Mongol rule included a lasting preference for centralized control and a more assertive imperial power, influencing later dynasties.

The Yuan Dynasty's approach to cultural interaction remains a subject of scholarly debate. While Kublai Khan is often credited with practicing **religious tolerance**, accommodating Buddhism, Taoism, Confucianism, and Islam, the reality was more nuanced. While religious freedoms were largely respected, the Mongol preference for Buddhism sometimes resulted in the marginalization of Confucian scholars, impacting the traditional role of Confucianism in governance.

Furthermore, the cultural exchange fostered by the Yuan Dynasty, particularly through the Silk Road, introduced new ideas, technologies, and artistic styles into China. However, the influx of foreign influences also led to *cultural clashes and social tensions*. The integration of Mongol and Chinese cultures was never fully achieved, resulting in a persisting sense of difference between the ruling elite and the Chinese population. This tension significantly contributed to the eventual downfall of the Yuan Dynasty.

The legal and social structures implemented by the Yuan Dynasty also had significant long-term consequences. The introduction of Mongol legal codes and administrative practices, while initially disruptive, laid the groundwork for future legal and administrative reforms. The Yuan legal system attempted to harmonize Mongol and Chinese laws, but the ultimate result was a complex hybrid system that contributed to bureaucratic inefficiencies. Moreover, the social hierarchy established by the Mongols, which placed them at the top and often discriminated against the Chinese population, left a lasting legacy of social inequality and resentment.

In conclusion, the long-term effects of Yuan policies on Chinese society were complex and far-reaching. While Kublai Khan's rule brought periods of economic prosperity and facilitated significant cultural exchange, it also resulted in social tensions, economic instability, and a lasting impact on China's administrative and legal systems. The Yuan Dynasty's legacy is a testament to the intricate interplay of conquest, adaptation, and the enduring resilience of Chinese culture in the face of significant historical change. The integration of Mongol and Chinese elements was partial and uneven, leaving a complex tapestry of influences that shaped the trajectory of subsequent Chinese dynasties. The aftermath of Mongol rule played a significant role in shaping China's political, economic, and cultural landscape for centuries to come.

15. The Silk Road's Flourishing Under Yuan Rule

Increased trade and cultural exchange along the Silk Road.

The reign of Kublai Khan witnessed a remarkable flourishing of the Silk Road, transforming it into a vibrant artery of commerce and cultural exchange that connected East and West like never before. This wasn't merely a continuation of existing trade routes; it represented a conscious and strategic effort by the Yuan Dynasty to leverage the Silk Road for economic prosperity and political influence.

Under Kublai Khan's rule, the Pax Mongolica, a period of relative peace and stability across vast swathes of Eurasia, created a secure environment for merchants and travelers. This relative peace, enforced by the might of the Mongol Empire, significantly reduced the risks associated with traversing the Silk Road, encouraging greater participation from diverse traders. Previously perilous stretches of the route became safer, leading to a dramatic increase in the volume of goods exchanged.

The Yuan Dynasty implemented policies explicitly designed to facilitate trade along the Silk Road. These included the establishment of post stations for relaying messages and providing assistance to travelers, the construction and maintenance of roads and bridges along major routes, and the standardization of weights and measures to streamline transactions. These infrastructural improvements, combined with the relatively stable political climate, created a more efficient and reliable trade network.

The expansion of trade brought not only material goods but also a significant influx of ideas and cultural practices. Merchants from various regions – Persia, Central Asia, the Middle East, Europe, and beyond – brought with them their languages, religions, art forms, and technologies. This created a melting pot of cultures in major cities like Khanbaliq (modern-day Beijing), where merchants and travelers from diverse backgrounds interacted, exchanged knowledge, and introduced new customs and beliefs.

One striking example of this cultural exchange is the presence of Marco Polo at the court of Kublai Khan. Polo's extensive travels and detailed accounts of the Yuan court and the Silk Road provided Europeans with a window into a world previously largely unknown. His descriptions of the immense wealth and diverse cultures of the East stimulated European interest in trade with the East, contributing to the age of exploration.

Beyond Marco Polo, numerous other travelers and traders journeyed along the Silk Road during the Yuan Dynasty, each carrying with them stories, goods, and ideas. This exchange contributed to a dynamic period of cultural synthesis, with the integration of foreign elements into Yuan culture and vice versa. The diffusion of artistic styles, religious practices, and technological innovations resulted in a unique blend of cultures that enriched both the East and the West.

The economic impact of this increased trade was considerable. The Yuan Dynasty benefitted immensely from the increased tax revenue generated by the thriving trade along the Silk Road. This wealth fueled the construction of grand infrastructure projects, supported the arts, and enhanced the power and prestige of the empire. The Silk Road's prosperity under Kublai Khan, therefore, wasn't merely an economic phenomenon; it was a crucial component of the Yuan Dynasty's success and its lasting legacy.

However, it is important to acknowledge that the prosperity of the Silk Road under Kublai Khan was not without its drawbacks. The exploitation of local populations for the purposes of trade and the imposition of a centralized system of administration did not always benefit all. Nevertheless, the heightened trade and cultural exchange along the Silk Road during this period remain a testament to the ambitious scope of Kublai Khan's reign and his vision for a unified and prosperous empire.

The legacy of the Silk Road during the Yuan Dynasty is profound. It represents a pivotal moment in global history, demonstrating the potential for trade to drive both economic growth and cultural exchange on an unprecedented scale. The interconnectedness fostered by the Silk Road under Kublai Khan left an indelible mark on the cultures and societies of Eurasia, shaping the world we know today.

The Impact of the Yuan Dynasty on Global Trade and Connectivity

The reign of Kublai Khan and the subsequent Yuan Dynasty profoundly reshaped the landscape of global trade and connectivity, leaving an indelible mark on the world's economic and cultural interactions. This impact stemmed from a confluence of factors, including deliberate imperial policies, the leveraging of pre-existing trade routes, and the inherent dynamism of the Mongol Empire itself.

Prior to the Yuan Dynasty, the Silk Road, while a crucial artery of commerce, faced challenges in consistency and security. The **fragmented political landscape** of Central Asia often resulted in disruptions and increased risks for merchants. However, the Mongol conquests under Kublai Khan's predecessors brought a degree of unprecedented political stability across a vast swathe of Eurasia. This newly unified and comparatively peaceful environment significantly enhanced the safety and reliability of trade routes, encouraging a dramatic **increase in the volume and diversity of goods exchanged**.

Kublai Khan actively fostered this economic expansion. Recognizing the immense potential of trade to enrich his empire, he implemented policies aimed at bolstering commerce. **Improved infrastructure**, such as the repair and extension of existing roads and the construction of new canals, facilitated the smoother movement of goods. The establishment of postal relay stations, the Yam, further streamlined communication and transportation across the empire, enhancing the efficiency of trade networks.

The Yuan Dynasty witnessed an **unprecedented flourishing of the Silk Road**. Goods flowed freely between the East and the West, with Chinese silks, porcelain, and tea reaching Europe in far greater quantities than before. Conversely, European textiles, glassware, and precious metals found their way to the East. This exchange was not limited to material goods; ideas, technologies, and religious beliefs also circulated along these trade routes, fostering unprecedented cultural exchange and integration.

The presence of numerous foreign merchants and envoys in Khanbaliq, the Yuan capital, underscored the cosmopolitan nature of this era.

The **economic policies of the Yuan Dynasty** further amplified these effects. The government actively promoted trade by reducing tariffs and simplifying customs procedures. The use of paper money and the standardization of weights and measures further facilitated transactions and trade across the vast expanse of the empire. Moreover, the relative peace and stability that characterized much of the Yuan period allowed for the establishment of more robust and reliable trade networks, which directly improved connectivity across continents.

The Yuan Dynasty's impact extended beyond the Silk Road. Maritime trade also experienced a significant boost. Chinese maritime technologies continued to advance, allowing for greater voyages across the Indian Ocean. The presence of Chinese traders and ships in Southeast Asia and even parts of the African coast testifies to the expanding reach of Yuan maritime trade. This expansion connected distant regions and facilitated the movement of goods and ideas across vast distances, fostering a more interconnected global economy.

However, it's crucial to acknowledge that this period of flourishing trade was not without its challenges. The high cost of administration, excessive taxation in some areas, and the eventual weakening of central authority all contributed to a decline in trade towards the later years of the dynasty. Despite these challenges, the **legacy of the Yuan Dynasty's impact on global trade and connectivity** remains substantial. The period laid the groundwork for subsequent centuries of increased interaction and exchange between the East and West, fundamentally changing the flow of goods, ideas, and cultures across Eurasia.

In conclusion, the Yuan Dynasty under Kublai Khan represents a pivotal moment in the history of global connectivity. The conscious policies enacted by the Yuan, combined with the overall security and stability fostered by Mongol rule, resulted in a period of unprecedented growth in trade along established routes and the expansion of maritime commerce. This period laid the foundations for a more interconnected world, significantly impacting global cultural exchange and economic development for centuries to come.

The legacy of the Silk Road during the Yuan period.

The Yuan dynasty, under the shrewd leadership of Kublai Khan, witnessed a remarkable resurgence of the Silk Road, transforming it from a network of disparate trade routes into a dynamic artery connecting East and West like never before. This revitalization wasn't merely a matter of increased trade volume; it represented a profound cultural and economic shift with lasting global consequences.

Kublai Khan's reign saw a deliberate policy of promoting trade and fostering connections along the Silk Road. This wasn't simply a matter of laissez-faire economics; rather, it was a conscious strategy to consolidate power and resources, integrating diverse cultures under his dominion. The emperor's emphasis on infrastructure development played a pivotal role. The construction and maintenance of roads, bridges, and canals facilitated the movement of goods and people, significantly reducing transit times and costs. This created a more secure and efficient trade network, encouraging merchants from across Eurasia to participate.

The Pax Mongolica, the relative peace and stability achieved under Mongol rule, was a crucial factor. The relative security along the Silk Road, reduced banditry, and a unified system of laws and currency promoted safe passage for traders. This reduced the risks associated with long-distance commerce, incentivizing greater investment and participation. The economic benefits were immense, as the free flow of goods and services led to unprecedented levels of prosperity in various cities along the trade routes. The capital, Khanbaliq (modern-day Beijing), flourished as a cosmopolitan hub bustling with merchants, artisans, and diplomats from diverse cultural backgrounds.

Beyond material goods, the Silk Road facilitated a significant exchange of ideas and cultural practices during the Yuan period. Religions like Buddhism, Islam, Christianity, and even Nestorianism found fertile ground in this multicultural environment. This led to a fascinating blend of traditions, fostering religious tolerance and mutual understanding, albeit not without tension. Artistic styles, culinary customs, and even technological innovations traveled along the trade routes, enriching the cultures of the participating societies. The exchange of intellectual ideas—philosophical concepts, scientific advancements, and literary works—also enriched the intellectual landscape of the age.

The legacy of the Silk Road during the Yuan period is a complex one. While undoubtedly enriching in many ways, it's important to acknowledge the challenges that accompanied this period of intensified trade. The sheer scale of the Mongol Empire, while fostering economic integration, also presented challenges in terms of administration and governance. The extraction of resources and taxation policies had varying impacts on different societies, some benefiting while others suffered. The rise of powerful merchant families and the occasional exploitation of local populations must also be considered when evaluating the full impact of the Yuan period's Silk Road.

However, the long-term effects are undeniable. The increased connectivity and cultural exchange during this era left a lasting mark on Eurasia. It stimulated innovation, spread knowledge, and fostered a globalized network that laid the groundwork for future interactions between East and West. The legacy of the Silk Road under Yuan rule highlights the power of trade and communication not just in fostering economic growth, but also in shaping cultural identities and transforming the very fabric of societies across continents. **The Yuan dynasty's influence on the Silk Road stands as a pivotal moment in world history, a testament to Kublai Khan's vision and the transformative potential of international exchange.**

16. Kublai Khan's Influence on Global History

The Impact of the Mongol Empire Under Kublai Khan on Global Affairs

Kublai Khan's reign as the fifth Khagan of the Mongol Empire, and the founder of the Yuan dynasty, indelibly shaped global affairs, leaving a legacy that resonates even today. His rule marked a pivotal moment in the interconnectedness of Eurasia, profoundly influencing trade, cultural exchange, and the geopolitical landscape.

The most immediate impact was the <u>expansion and consolidation</u> of the Mongol Empire's vast territory. Under Kublai Khan, the empire reached its zenith, encompassing a significant portion of Eurasia, from modern-day China to parts of Southeast Asia, Russia, and the Middle East. This unprecedented geographical reach facilitated unprecedented levels of interconnectedness, creating a relatively stable and secure environment for trade and travel along the **Silk Road**. The <u>Pax Mongolica,</u> a period of relative peace and stability enforced by the Mongol Empire's military dominance, fostered a flourishing of commerce, enabling the free flow of goods, ideas, and technologies across continents. This facilitated the transmission of knowledge, religious beliefs, and artistic styles, creating a unique era of cultural exchange.

Kublai Khan's reign witnessed a dramatic increase in trade along the Silk Road. The unified administration and security provided by the Mongol Empire reduced the risks associated with long-distance trade, thereby encouraging merchants from across Europe, the Middle East, and Asia to travel and trade more freely. The resulting increase in commerce boosted the economies of the various regions within the empire and beyond, contributing to increased wealth and prosperity. This expanded trade is evident in the accounts of travelers such as *Marco Polo*, whose chronicles vividly depict the vibrant commercial centers and sophisticated trade networks within the empire. The flow of goods extended beyond material items; technological innovations and agricultural techniques were also exchanged, leading to advancements in various sectors across Eurasia.

Beyond economics, Kublai Khan's empire significantly influenced cultural exchange. His policy of relative religious tolerance allowed for the coexistence of various faiths, including Buddhism, Taoism, Confucianism, Islam, and Christianity. This created a unique environment of cultural blending, evident in the architectural styles, artistic expressions, and philosophical ideas that flourished within his court. The influx of foreign merchants and scholars brought new ideas and traditions, enriching the intellectual and artistic landscape of the empire. The fusion of Mongol and Chinese cultures, in particular, created a new synthesis that left a lasting impact on Chinese culture and identity.

However, Kublai Khan's impact on global affairs was not solely positive. The Mongol Empire's military might, while fostering trade and relative peace within its vast boundaries, also led to conquests and devastation in many regions. His military campaigns, such as the failed invasions of Japan and attempts to conquer Southeast Asian kingdoms, showcased both the ambition and limitations of Mongol power. These military actions, while unsuccessful in many respects, still disrupted existing regional powers and influenced the political dynamics of the regions involved. The constant threat of Mongol expansion shaped the foreign policies of many neighboring states, prompting them to either align with or resist the empire's dominance.

In conclusion, the impact of Kublai Khan's reign on global affairs was multifaceted and far-reaching. While his empire brought a period of relative peace and unprecedented interconnectedness through the expansion of trade along the Silk Road and a unique era of cultural exchange, it also resulted in military conflict and upheaval in many regions. His legacy serves as a complex and compelling example of the potential both for constructive and destructive impact on a global scale, demonstrating the profound and lasting consequences of empires on the course of world history.

The Lasting Effects of Mongol Expansion on Eurasia.

The Mongol conquests under Genghis Khan and his successors, including Kublai Khan, irrevocably reshaped the political, economic, and cultural landscape of Eurasia. The empire's vast expanse, stretching from East Asia to Eastern Europe, facilitated unprecedented levels of interconnectedness, yet also left a legacy of both destruction and innovation. Understanding these lasting effects requires a nuanced examination of the diverse regions impacted and the multifaceted nature of Mongol rule.

One of the most significant consequences was the promotion of trade and cultural exchange along established and newly forged routes. The Pax Mongolica, a period of relative peace and stability within the empire, allowed for the safe passage of merchants and travelers along the Silk Road and other trade networks. This facilitated the exchange of goods, ideas, and technologies across continents. *Spices, textiles, and porcelain* flowed westward from Asia, while European goods, including *silver and horses*, found their way eastward. This increased interaction between disparate cultures led to the diffusion of knowledge and artistic styles, leaving an indelible mark on the societies involved.

However, the Mongol expansion was not without its devastating consequences. The initial conquests were often marked by brutal violence and widespread destruction. Cities were razed, populations were slaughtered, and established political structures were overthrown. The **destruction of infrastructure and disruption of agricultural practices** led to widespread famine and economic hardship in many regions. The **long-term impact of this violence** varied depending on the region, but it undoubtedly shaped the demographic and socio-political realities of many Eurasian societies for generations to come.

The Mongol conquests also had a profound **impact on political structures**. While the Mongols initially relied on existing administrative systems in conquered territories, they gradually implemented their own forms of governance. This often involved the creation of new administrative divisions and the appointment of Mongol officials, which led to a degree of political centralization across vast regions. However, this centralized authority was often fragile, and the empire's vast size posed significant challenges for effective control. Internal rebellions and fragmentation were common throughout the Mongol empire's history.

The *legacy of Mongol rule on the political organization of Eurasia* is complex. While the empire ultimately fragmented, its influence on political thought and administrative practices persisted for centuries in the various successor states and the societies that emerged from its collapse. Many states adopted aspects of the Mongol military organization and administrative strategies. The experience of Mongol rule fostered new forms of diplomacy and interstate relations across Eurasia.

In the realm of cultural exchange, the Mongol period saw the transmission of ideas and practices between East and West. Religious beliefs, philosophical concepts, and artistic styles flowed across the vast empire, creating a unique blend of cultural influences. The interaction between Mongol and indigenous cultures produced syncretic religious practices, and artistic styles were often adapted and reinterpreted as they moved across Eurasia.

The **long-term effects of Mongol expansion on Eurasia** are multifaceted and continue to be debated by historians. While the initial conquests were often brutal and disruptive, the resulting period of interconnectedness facilitated unprecedented levels of cultural exchange and trade. The political structures established by the Mongols, though often unstable, left a lasting mark on the organization of many Eurasian states. The legacy of the Mongol empire is a complex tapestry woven from threads of violence, innovation, and exchange, forever altering the course of Eurasian history.

The Legacy of Kublai Khan's Rule on the Modern World

Kublai Khan's impact resonates far beyond the confines of his historical era, subtly shaping aspects of the modern world in ways that often go unnoticed. His reign, a complex tapestry woven from conquest, administration, and cultural exchange, left an enduring legacy that continues to influence our understanding of global history, political strategy, and cross-cultural interaction.

One of the most significant legacies is the <u>indirect influence on globalization</u>. While not a direct cause, Kublai Khan's promotion of the Silk Road during the Yuan Dynasty significantly facilitated trade and cultural exchange between East and West. This period of relative peace and connectivity, though ultimately temporary, laid the groundwork for future interactions, demonstrating the potential for global interconnectedness that only fully bloomed centuries later. The infrastructure improvements – roads, canals, and postal systems – fostered efficient trade routes and communication networks, precursors to the modern globalized economy.

Furthermore, Kublai Khan's **tolerance towards diverse religions** and cultures offers a powerful, albeit imperfect, model for modern multicultural societies. His Yuan court housed representatives from Buddhism, Taoism, Confucianism, Islam, and Christianity, fostering a complex religious and cultural landscape. Although instances of religious friction undoubtedly existed, his policy of religious tolerance stands in stark contrast to many periods of history marked by religious conflict and persecution. His example suggests the potential for peaceful coexistence in diverse societies, though the challenges of achieving such harmony remain.

His <u>administrative reforms</u> within the Yuan Dynasty, though tailored to a specific context, offer valuable insights into the complexities of governing a vast and diverse empire. His attempts to integrate Mongol and Chinese administrative structures, albeit with varying degrees of success, showcase the inherent challenges of balancing the needs of a dominant culture with those of a conquered population. Scholars today study his administrative strategies to understand the successes and failures of large-scale integration efforts, drawing parallels to contemporary issues of governance and multiculturalism.

Moreover, Kublai Khan's **military strategies** and campaigns, while often brutal, remain subject to extensive historical analysis. His strategic thinking, logistical prowess, and military innovations (even considering their ultimate failures in some instances, such as the invasion of Japan) are carefully studied by military historians and strategists. These studies, in turn, inform modern military theory and planning, highlighting the enduring value of studying past strategies, adapting them to contemporary conditions and, crucially, understanding their limitations.

Finally, *Kublai Khan's legacy extends to the realm of cultural and literary exchange.* The accounts of Marco Polo, though sometimes debated in terms of accuracy, profoundly influenced European perceptions of the East, igniting curiosity and shaping narratives about distant lands for centuries. This period's cultural exchanges left an indelible mark on both Eastern and Western cultures, illustrating the deep and far-reaching consequences of sustained cross-cultural interactions.

In conclusion, while **Kublai Khan's rule** was characterized by both remarkable achievements and undeniable brutality, its legacy continues to resonate in the modern world. His efforts toward globalization (in its nascent form), religious tolerance, administrative integration, military strategies, and cultural exchange offer scholars and policy-makers valuable lessons and cautionary tales. The analysis of his reign not only enriches our understanding of history but also provides a lens through which to examine contemporary challenges and possibilities in governance, cultural relations, and the intricate dance of global interconnectedness. The echoes of his empire still reverberate in the complex tapestry of our modern world.

17. Reassessing the Mongol-Chinese Integration

A Comprehensive Analysis of the Cultural and Societal Fusion During the Yuan Dynasty

The Yuan Dynasty, established by Kublai Khan in 1271, stands as a unique period in Chinese history, a time of unprecedented cultural and societal fusion. It was a complex interplay between the conquering Mongol forces and the established Chinese civilization, resulting in a dynamic synthesis that profoundly shaped the trajectory of both cultures.

The Mongol conquest wasn't simply a military takeover; it was a forceful introduction of nomadic pastoralist traditions into a sophisticated agrarian society. This clash of cultures initially manifested in tensions and resistance. The **Mongol elite**, with their distinct language, customs, and governance structures, largely maintained their separate identity within the Yuan court. They often favored positions of power and authority, leading to resentment among the Chinese population. However, the **length of the Yuan Dynasty's rule** (nearly a century) fostered an unavoidable process of interaction and exchange.

One key aspect of this fusion was the **administrative integration**. While the Yuan administration retained some

Mongol elements, it also adopted and adapted aspects of the established Chinese bureaucratic system. The Mongols, recognizing the efficiency and complexity of Chinese governance, gradually integrated Chinese officials into their administration. This led to a blend of administrative styles, where Mongol leadership was coupled with the expertise of experienced Chinese bureaucrats. This strategic blend allowed for effective rule across the vast empire while retaining a Mongol presence in pivotal leadership roles.

The **economic sphere** experienced considerable integration. While the Mongols initially imposed their own economic policies, they eventually recognized the benefits of integrating with the established Chinese economic systems. The flourishing **Silk Road** trade experienced a revitalization under Yuan rule, facilitating the exchange of not just goods but also ideas and cultural practices between East and West. The Yuan emperors actively promoted trade and commerce, fostering economic growth that benefited both Mongol and Chinese populations. This created a shared economic interest that transcended initial cultural divisions.

In the realm of culture, the fusion was perhaps most evident. While Mongol artistic styles and traditions initially held prominence in the Yuan court, a gradual blending occurred. Chinese artistic traditions, with their long history and refined techniques, continued to thrive, influencing Mongol aesthetics. This resulted in a hybrid art form that combined Mongol dynamism with the elegance and sophistication of Chinese art. Architectural marvels like the capital city of Khanbaliq (modern-day Beijing) exemplified this cultural fusion, demonstrating a blend of Mongol and Chinese architectural styles.

Furthermore, the *religious landscape* under the Yuan witnessed remarkable tolerance. While Tibetan Buddhism enjoyed imperial patronage, other faiths, including Taoism, Confucianism, Islam, and Christianity, coexisted relatively peacefully. This religious tolerance, albeit not always perfectly implemented, facilitated cultural exchange and promoted a more inclusive societal environment. The interaction between these diverse religious traditions contributed to a unique spiritual climate, influencing philosophical thought and societal values.

However, the integration was not without its challenges. The Mongol conquest caused considerable upheaval and suffering among the Chinese population. The social hierarchy remained heavily skewed in favor of the Mongols, fueling resentment and resistance. While economic prosperity increased for some, many Chinese felt marginalized and exploited by the ruling class. These tensions contributed to rebellions and ultimately to the downfall of the Yuan Dynasty.

In conclusion, the Yuan Dynasty represents a complex and multifaceted period of **cultural and societal fusion**. While initially marked by conflict and dominance, the prolonged interaction between Mongol and Chinese cultures led to a remarkable synthesis. The Yuan period demonstrates that even under conditions of conquest, cultural exchange and integration can occur, albeit with profound and long-lasting consequences for both societies involved. The legacy of the Yuan Dynasty remains a testament to the dynamic, and sometimes turbulent, nature of cultural interaction throughout history. Its analysis offers invaluable insights into the intricate processes of cultural exchange, adaptation, and the enduring impact of intercultural contact on the shaping of civilizations.

Examining the Lasting Effects of This Integration on China's Identity.

The Mongol conquest of China under Kublai Khan, while initially marked by upheaval and resistance, ultimately initiated a period of profound cultural and societal fusion that irrevocably shaped the course of Chinese history and identity. Understanding the lasting effects of this integration requires examining its multifaceted impact across various spheres of Chinese life: political, economic, social, and cultural.

Politically, the Yuan Dynasty's establishment under a foreign ruler undeniably challenged the established Chinese imperial order. The **Mongol administrative system**, initially alien to Chinese traditions, gradually integrated with existing structures. While the Mongols maintained a distinct administrative hierarchy, the **adoption of Chinese bureaucratic practices and legal codes** became increasingly prevalent, demonstrating a pragmatic adaptation rather than a complete imposition of foreign rule. This pragmatic integration, while initially causing friction, ultimately **laid the groundwork for future dynasties** to synthesize elements of both Mongol and Chinese administrative styles.

Economically, the Yuan Dynasty witnessed a period of both disruption and expansion. The **extensive trade networks** established by the Mongols along the Silk Road spurred unprecedented economic growth. The influx of foreign merchants and the promotion of international trade enriched China's economy and introduced new goods and technologies. However, this economic boom was not evenly distributed, and it coexisted with existing economic systems and inequalities. **The integration of Mongol and Chinese economic practices** resulted in a complex interplay of traditional Chinese mercantile structures and new, expansive trade routes, ultimately bolstering China's global economic presence.

Socially, the Mongol conquest disrupted traditional Chinese social hierarchies. While the Mongols initially occupied the upper echelons of society, a gradual integration of Mongol and Chinese elites occurred over time. **Intermarriage between Mongol and Chinese families** became increasingly common, leading to a blurring of social boundaries. While significant social stratification persisted, the **interaction and mixing of different ethnic groups** contributed to a gradually evolving social landscape, albeit one characterized by both cooperation and conflict.

Culturally, the integration of Mongol and Chinese traditions resulted in a unique cultural synthesis. While the Yuan Dynasty maintained a preference for Mongol customs and practices, it also **actively patronized Chinese art, literature, and scholarship**. This resulted in a remarkable exchange of ideas and artistic styles, blending Mongol nomadic aesthetics with sophisticated Chinese artistic traditions. **The fusion of Buddhist, Daoist, Confucian, and Islamic beliefs** under a policy of religious tolerance further enriched the religious landscape. This cultural exchange, though marked by instances of appropriation and resistance, ultimately contributed to a uniquely blended cultural identity that would endure long after the Yuan Dynasty's collapse.

In conclusion, the integration of Mongol and Chinese cultures during the Yuan Dynasty profoundly and permanently altered China's identity. While the initial conquest was undeniably disruptive, the resulting synthesis fostered a unique blend of political systems, economic practices, social structures, and cultural expressions. This **cultural fusion, marked by both conflict and collaboration,** laid the groundwork for a more interconnected and globally engaged China, shaping its identity in ways that resonate even today. The legacy of the Yuan Dynasty is not merely one of conquest and rule, but of a transformative cultural exchange that permanently altered the trajectory of Chinese history and its conception of itself on the world stage.

The Complex Relationship Between Mongol Conquerors and the Chinese Population

The Mongol conquest of China under Kublai Khan marked a pivotal moment in history, initiating a period of complex and often contradictory interactions between the conquering Mongols and the conquered Chinese population. This relationship, far from being a simple story of oppression and resistance, was characterized by a nuanced interplay of power dynamics, cultural exchange, and evolving societal structures.

Initially, the relationship was undeniably one of domination. The Mongols, a nomadic people with a distinct culture and social organization, imposed their rule upon the sophisticated and established Chinese civilization. This led to **initial resistance** and resentment among segments of the Chinese population, who viewed the Mongol rulers as foreign invaders disrupting their way of life. Many scholars and officials refused to collaborate with the new regime, leading to periods of conflict and unrest. The imposition of Mongol customs and laws, often at odds with established Chinese traditions, further fueled these tensions. <u>Systematic discrimination</u> against the Chinese population in favor of Mongols and other favored groups was a hallmark of the early Yuan Dynasty. Access to power, wealth, and prestigious positions in government and society was often restricted based on ethnicity.

However, the story does not end with resistance alone. Over time, a process of gradual <u>integration</u> and **cultural exchange** began to unfold. Kublai Khan, despite his initial reliance on Mongol officials, recognized the need to incorporate Chinese expertise and knowledge to effectively govern the vast empire. He adopted many aspects of Chinese administration, utilizing existing bureaucratic systems and employing talented Chinese officials to assist in governance. This pragmatic approach, while sometimes driven by necessity, also reflects a degree of *adaptation* on the part of the Mongol rulers. The adoption of Chinese administrative structures and practices demonstrated a willingness to incorporate elements of the conquered culture into the functioning of the state.

The economic policies of the Yuan Dynasty also played a significant role in shaping the relationship between the two populations. The promotion of trade, particularly along the Silk Road, brought economic prosperity to certain segments of Chinese society and facilitated cross-cultural interactions. While the benefits of this prosperity were not evenly distributed, it nonetheless fostered a degree of interdependence between the Mongols and the Chinese. The flow of goods, ideas, and individuals across vast distances led to a gradual but significant exchange of cultural practices and beliefs.

Furthermore, Kublai Khan's policy of religious tolerance fostered a surprising level of co-existence between diverse religious and cultural groups within the empire. Buddhism, Taoism, Confucianism, Islam, and even Christianity found patrons among different segments of the population, both Mongol and Chinese. This, to a certain degree, softened the rigid ethnic hierarchies and fostered a climate of relative openness despite the underlying political power imbalance. Patronage of the arts and learning, regardless of ethnic origin, contributed to a unique blending of cultural influences, leaving a lasting legacy on Chinese art and literature.

Despite the positive developments, the relationship remained fraught with tension throughout the Yuan Dynasty. Rebellions and uprisings frequently erupted as the Chinese population resisted Mongol rule. These uprisings, while sometimes localized, often reflected deeper grievances stemming from ethnic discrimination, economic inequality, and cultural suppression. The Mongol response to these rebellions was often brutal, reinforcing feelings of resentment and opposition. The inherent inequality embedded within the system ensured that the relationship between conqueror and conquered remained fundamentally unbalanced, even as a degree of assimilation and cultural exchange occurred.

In conclusion, the relationship between the Mongol conquerors and the Chinese population under Kublai Khan was a complex and multifaceted tapestry woven from threads of domination, resistance, collaboration, and cultural exchange. While the initial phase was undeniably characterized by Mongol dominance and Chinese resistance, the Yuan Dynasty also witnessed a degree of integration and intermingling of cultures, leaving a lasting impact on both Chinese and Mongol societies. The legacy of this period continues to be debated and reinterpreted, reminding us of the intricate and often paradoxical nature of historical interactions between different cultures and societies.

18. Historiography of Kublai Khan: Diverse Perspectives

Examining the different historical accounts and interpretations of Kublai Khan's reign.

A Multifaceted Legacy: Deconstructing the Historical Narratives of Kublai Khan

The historical record surrounding Kublai Khan, the fifth Khagan of the Mongol Empire and founder of the Yuan dynasty, is remarkably rich yet profoundly complex. His reign, spanning from 1260 to 1294, witnessed unprecedented territorial expansion, significant cultural exchange, and ambitious infrastructural projects, all of which have fueled a multitude of interpretations throughout history. Understanding Kublai Khan requires navigating a labyrinth of diverse perspectives, shaped by the biases, agendas, and cultural backgrounds of the chroniclers who documented his era.

Early Mongol Chronicles offer a unique perspective, primarily focusing on the military accomplishments and lineage of the Khan. Works like the *Secret History of the Mongols*, while not directly focused on Kublai's reign, provide invaluable context regarding Mongol culture, military strategies, and the broader historical trajectory of the empire. These accounts often celebrate Kublai's military prowess and his successful conquest of Southern Song China, emphasizing his role as a continuation of the legacy of Genghis Khan, often framing his reign within the wider narrative of Mongol expansionism and imperial ambition. These early chronicles, however, are often short on details regarding internal administration and his dealings with the Chinese populace, creating a partial and potentially skewed image of his governance.

Chinese Perspectives, arising from both official Yuan Dynasty records and private accounts, offer a starkly different narrative. These sources, naturally, offer insights into the social and economic impact of Mongol rule on China. Some accounts highlight the significant disruptions caused by the conquest, the cultural clashes between the conquering Mongols and the conquered Chinese, and the imposition of Mongol governance structures on a deeply ingrained Chinese bureaucratic system. While some acknowledge Kublai Khan's efforts towards integrating Mongol and Chinese cultures, particularly in economic and administrative policies, these sources often express resentment toward Mongol rule and its perceived disruptions to traditional Chinese society. The **construction of Khanbaliq (Beijing)**, while celebrated as a symbol of Yuan power and cultural exchange by some, is seen by others as a potent symbol of Mongol dominance and the suppression of Chinese identity.

Marco Polo's account, arguably the most famous Western narrative about Kublai Khan's reign, introduces another layer of complexity. *Polo's Travels, written decades after his return from the East*, provides a vivid portrayal of the Yuan court and the scale of the empire, capturing the exoticism and wonder of the East for a European audience. However, the veracity of Polo's accounts remains a subject of scholarly debate. Some scholars argue that Polo's descriptions, albeit entertaining, are exaggerated or fabricated, while others defend their accuracy based on archaeological findings and corroborative evidence from other sources. This divergence in interpretation highlights the need for careful scrutiny and cross-referencing when relying on this iconic source.

Later Historical Writings, produced centuries after the Yuan dynasty's fall, draw from a wider range of sources and offer more nuanced perspectives. These accounts often take a more critical view of the Mongol empire, recognizing its successes alongside its brutality, its advancements as well as its destructiveness. Historians have delved into the complexities of Mongol rule, attempting to balance their assessment of Kublai Khan's legacy, acknowledging both his achievements in promoting economic growth and cultural exchange, and the undeniable suffering inflicted upon the Chinese population under his rule. These later analyses benefit from the hindsight afforded by centuries of scholarship and a greater understanding of the socio-political context of the Yuan dynasty.

In conclusion, the historical accounts of Kublai Khan's reign are not monolithic but rather a tapestry woven from diverse perspectives, each shaped by its own unique biases and limitations. By examining these varying interpretations, comparing and contrasting the accounts of Mongol, Chinese, and Western chroniclers, and carefully evaluating the veracity and context of their narratives, a more complete and nuanced understanding of Kublai Khan's multifaceted legacy emerges. It is through this critical analysis of a multitude of voices that we can hope to truly grasp the complexities of his reign and his enduring impact on global history.

Analyzing the biases and perspectives of various historians throughout history.

The historiography of Kublai Khan reveals a fascinating interplay of perspectives, shaped by the cultural contexts, political agendas, and available sources of the historians themselves. A nuanced understanding requires acknowledging these inherent biases and examining how they influenced interpretations of his reign.

Early accounts, often penned by contemporary chroniclers within the Yuan Dynasty or neighboring states, frequently reflected the political climate of their time. Chinese historians, for instance, might emphasize the impact of Kublai Khan's rule on Chinese society, highlighting both the positive aspects of economic growth and infrastructure development and the negative aspects of Mongol dominance and cultural imposition. Their narratives might reflect a lingering resentment towards foreign rule or a desire to portray a resilient Chinese identity surviving under duress. Conversely, Mongol accounts could focus on the military achievements and expansion of the empire under Kublai Khan, emphasizing his legitimacy as a successor to Genghis Khan and the greatness of the Mongol empire. These narratives often downplayed or omitted accounts of brutality or resistance from conquered peoples.

The arrival of Marco Polo and the subsequent dissemination of his accounts in Europe introduced a new layer of perspective. While Polo's descriptions of Kublai Khan's court were influential in shaping Western perceptions of the East, they were not without bias. Written from the perspective of a Venetian merchant, Polo's account emphasizes trade and commerce, portraying Kublai Khan as a powerful, wealthy, and sophisticated ruler. However, his narrative omits many crucial aspects of Yuan politics and society, possibly due to limited access or deliberate choices to focus on aspects that served his purposes. Later European historians often relied heavily on Polo's accounts, perpetuating a particular image of Kublai Khan that may not fully reflect the complexity of his reign.

The 19th and 20th centuries saw the emergence of more critical and scholarly approaches to the study of Kublai Khan. Historians began to reassess the available sources, recognizing the limitations and biases within individual narratives. Modern scholarship has benefited from the discovery and translation of a wider range of primary sources, including previously neglected Chinese and Mongol texts. This has allowed for a more balanced understanding of Kublai Khan, moving beyond simplistic characterizations as either a benevolent ruler or a ruthless conqueror.

Modern historians also grapple with questions of cultural translation and interpretation. The challenge lies in interpreting sources written in different languages and cultural contexts, ensuring that translations accurately reflect the original meaning and intent. Moreover, historians must contend with the inherent difficulties of understanding the perspectives of individuals from vastly different historical periods and cultural backgrounds.

In conclusion, the historiography of Kublai Khan is a rich and multifaceted landscape. Understanding his reign demands careful consideration of the biases inherent in historical sources, awareness of the political and cultural contexts shaping these accounts, and a commitment to seeking out and integrating a wide range of perspectives. By critically examining these biases, we can move towards a more complete and nuanced understanding of one of history's most enigmatic figures.

- A Professional Historian

Presenting a Balanced Overview of Different Interpretations and Historical Narratives.

The historiography of Kublai Khan, a pivotal figure bridging East and West, is rich and multifaceted, reflecting the evolving perspectives of historians across centuries. Understanding his legacy necessitates navigating a complex tapestry of interpretations, each shaped by its own historical context and biases.

Early accounts, often colored by the experiences of travelers like Marco Polo, tended to romanticize Kublai Khan's court, portraying a sophisticated and powerful emperor presiding over a thriving empire. Polo's influential travelogue, while undeniably a significant source, must be approached cautiously. Recent scholarship highlights the potential exaggerations and inaccuracies within his narratives, prompting a reassessment of his descriptions of opulence and grandeur.

Conversely, Chinese historical accounts, often written from the perspective of the conquered Song dynasty elite, frequently portray Kublai Khan in a less favorable light. These narratives emphasize the destructive aspects of the Mongol conquest, highlighting the loss of traditional Chinese culture and the imposition of foreign rule. Such sources offer critical counterpoints to the more romanticized Western perspectives, emphasizing the disruption and suffering endured by the Chinese population under Mongol dominance.

More recent scholarship has attempted to move beyond these polarized views, offering a more nuanced and balanced understanding of Kublai Khan's reign. Historians are increasingly emphasizing the complex interplay of Mongol and Chinese cultures during the Yuan dynasty, acknowledging both the destruction and the creative synthesis that characterized this era. This approach recognizes the significant administrative reforms and infrastructure projects undertaken during Kublai's rule, as well as the relative tolerance afforded to various religious groups.

Furthermore, modern historians are increasingly examining the economic and social transformations that occurred under Kublai's leadership. The impact of his policies on trade along the Silk Road, the development of a centralized bureaucracy, and the promotion of intercultural exchange are receiving more in-depth analysis. This has led to a more comprehensive understanding of the long-term consequences of his rule, both positive and negative.

The study of Kublai Khan's reign is not merely a matter of recounting historical events; it involves interpreting complex interactions between different cultures, assessing the reliability of various sources, and considering the long-term consequences of his actions. This requires a critical engagement with diverse perspectives, moving beyond simplistic narratives of heroism or villainy to appreciate the multifaceted nature of his legacy. It is through this ongoing process of critical examination and reassessment that we can gain a more complete and balanced understanding of Kublai Khan's enduring influence on global history.

By synthesizing various accounts – from Marco Polo's adventurous tales to the more sober assessments of Chinese chronicles and modern scholarly interpretations – we can craft a richer, more complete narrative. This multifaceted approach allows for a balanced appraisal of Kublai Khan's accomplishments, his failings, and the lasting impact of his rule on the cultural landscape of Eurasia and beyond. The ongoing scholarly debate concerning his legacy underscores the complexity of his reign and the richness of its historical interpretations.

Ultimately, the most compelling historical narratives about Kublai Khan are those that engage critically with the available sources, acknowledge the biases inherent in each perspective, and present a nuanced and thought-provoking analysis of his life and reign. This approach allows future generations to learn not only the facts of his story but also the methods by which we arrive at a meaningful understanding of the past.

19. The Enduring Myths and Legends of Kublai Khan

Exploring the popular culture and folklore surrounding Kublai Khan's life and reign.

The historical figure of Kublai Khan, the fifth Khagan of the Mongol Empire and founder of the Yuan dynasty, transcends the dusty pages of history books, weaving itself into the vibrant tapestry of popular culture and folklore. His image, far from being static, has evolved and adapted across centuries, reflecting the changing perceptions and needs of different societies.

One of the most pervasive portrayals stems from Marco Polo's **travelogue**. While debated for its accuracy, Polo's vivid descriptions of Kublai Khan's magnificent court in **Khanbaliq** (modern-day Beijing) – a city of unparalleled opulence and sophistication – significantly shaped Western perceptions. This image of a powerful, wise, and cosmopolitan emperor, surrounded by exotic riches and advanced technology, became deeply ingrained in the European imagination. It fueled countless stories and artistic depictions, establishing a foundation for Kublai Khan's legendary status in Western lore.

In contrast, **East Asian narratives** often present a more nuanced and complex picture. While acknowledging his imperial power and accomplishments in unifying China, these accounts also highlight the challenges and internal conflicts of his reign. The *resistance to Mongol rule* and the dynasty's eventual decline are frequently featured, offering a counterpoint to the more romanticized Western perspective. This is particularly visible in Chinese literature and theater, where Kublai Khan is often presented as a figure both imposing and ultimately vulnerable, a potent symbol of both imperial grandeur and the transience of power.

The **legend of Kublai Khan** also extends beyond traditional historical narratives. He has become a recurring character in popular fiction, often appearing in fantasy novels, historical dramas, and video games. These depictions frequently exaggerate or embellish certain aspects of his life, transforming him into a larger-than-life figure. Sometimes he's presented as a benevolent but ultimately flawed ruler, while in others he's depicted as a ruthless conqueror. The interpretations are as diverse as the media themselves.

Furthermore, the *myths and legends* associated with Kublai Khan often involve elements of magic and supernatural power. In some stories, he possesses uncanny foresight, while in others he is associated with mythical creatures or possesses magical artifacts. These fantastical elements further cement his image as a figure far removed from ordinary mortality, a testament to his lasting impact on the collective imagination.

The **persistence of Kublai Khan's legend** in popular culture underscores his significant role in global history. His influence extended far beyond the political boundaries of the Yuan dynasty. The stories told about him, whether factual or fictional, reveal the enduring human fascination with power, empire, and the intersection of different cultures. His image continues to evolve, reflecting the ongoing attempts to understand not only the historical Kublai Khan but also the complex and ever-shifting narratives that have shaped his enduring legacy.

Moreover, the **varied portrayals of Kublai Khan** highlight the subjective nature of historical interpretation. The same figure can be viewed as a wise and benevolent ruler or a ruthless conqueror depending on the perspective and the context. These diverse narratives provide valuable insights into the cultural values and biases of the societies that have embraced, adapted, and reinterpreted the story of this remarkable emperor.

Ultimately, the folklore surrounding Kublai Khan is a testament to the enduring fascination with this monumental figure. The stories, legends, and adaptations demonstrate not just his historical significance but also the powerful role that mythmaking plays in shaping our understanding of the past and the enduring influence of historical figures on the present.

Analyzing the evolution of these myths and legends throughout history.

The legacy of Kublai Khan, a figure straddling the vast expanse of Mongol conquest and the sophisticated culture of China, has been woven into a rich tapestry of myths and legends. These narratives, passed down through generations, reflect not only the historical reality of his reign but also the evolving societal values and perspectives of those who inherited his story. Understanding their evolution reveals a fascinating interplay between fact, fiction, and cultural interpretation.

Early accounts, often penned by those within the Yuan court or those who had direct contact with the empire, tend to **emphasize Kublai Khan's imperial power and administrative prowess**. These narratives, while sometimes embellished, often focused on his monumental building projects, his ambitious military campaigns (even when unsuccessful, like the invasion of Japan), and his attempts to forge a unified empire encompassing diverse cultures. Marco Polo's chronicles, for instance, while not entirely without bias, offered a vivid, albeit romanticized, portrayal of Kublai Khan's court, emphasizing its opulence and the emperor's apparent wisdom and tolerance.

However, as time progressed, the myths surrounding Kublai Khan began to diverge from purely political narratives. **The Ming Dynasty, which overthrew the Yuan, naturally presented a less flattering image.** Their accounts often downplayed Kublai Khan's accomplishments while highlighting the perceived brutality and foreignness of Mongol rule. This served a propagandistic purpose, solidifying the legitimacy of the Ming and presenting a narrative of restoring a uniquely Chinese identity.

In later centuries, the legend of Kublai Khan continued to evolve, absorbing elements of Chinese folklore and popular storytelling. He became a figure imbued with both grandeur and tragedy, **a potent symbol of imperial ambition tempered by the limitations of human power**. The stories shifted in focus, incorporating elements of romance, magic, and even supernatural encounters. These narratives were often rooted in regional variations, creating a diverse landscape of mythical tales centered around the same historical figure.

The **20th and 21st centuries witnessed a renewed interest in Kublai Khan, fueled by both scholarly research and popular culture**. Modern historians have strived to disentangle fact from fiction, utilizing a wider range of sources and methodologies to provide a more nuanced understanding of his life and reign. Yet, even modern interpretations often acknowledge the enduring power of the myths and legends, recognizing their significance in shaping cultural perceptions. Movies, novels, and video games have all drawn upon this rich reservoir of stories, creating their own interpretations that blend historical accuracy with creative license.

The *evolution of Kublai Khan's image, therefore, reveals not just the passage of time, but also the ever-shifting sands of cultural memory*. The narratives surrounding him are not merely historical artifacts; they are living testaments to the enduring power of storytelling and the ways in which societies make sense of their past. His legacy, as reflected in the myths and legends, becomes a mirror reflecting the values, anxieties, and aspirations of each generation that inherited his story.

It is within this dynamic interplay between history, myth, and popular culture that we can truly appreciate the complexity of Kublai Khan's lasting impact. The stories continue to evolve, mirroring the ongoing dialogue between past and present.

Examining how these myths have shaped perceptions of Kublai Khan's legacy.

The legacy of Kublai Khan, a figure of immense historical significance, has been profoundly shaped by the myths and legends that have accumulated around his life and reign. These narratives, passed down through generations, often diverge from historical accuracy, yet they powerfully influence how we understand his impact on the world.

One persistent myth portrays Kublai Khan as a benevolent and wise ruler, a patron of the arts and a champion of cultural exchange. This image is fueled by accounts like those of Marco Polo, who depicted a magnificent court brimming with riches and sophistication. While Kublai Khan undoubtedly fostered trade and sponsored cultural interaction along the Silk Road, this romanticized portrayal often overshadows the harsh realities of his rule, including military conquests, the suppression of rebellions, and the immense human cost of his empire's expansion. The positive aspects of his reign are frequently amplified, while the less palatable truths are downplayed, shaping a legacy that emphasizes his achievements over his less glorious actions.

Conversely, other myths paint Kublai Khan as a cruel and ruthless tyrant, a bloodthirsty conqueror who employed brutal methods to maintain his power. This perspective often arises from accounts emphasizing the Mongol conquests and their devastating impact on conquered populations. The massacres and destruction wrought by the Mongol armies are vividly recounted, fueling a narrative that centers on the violence and oppression inherent in his rule. This interpretation tends to focus on the negative aspects of his legacy, often minimizing his administrative reforms and cultural achievements in favor of highlighting the empire's inherent brutality. This biased presentation shapes a legacy built upon fear and aggression, neglecting the complex nuances of his leadership.

The enduring power of these contrasting myths underscores the inherent subjectivity in historical interpretations. The very act of storytelling, even when rooted in documented facts, inevitably involves selection and emphasis, shaping the final narrative. The absence of a single, universally accepted account of Kublai Khan's life allows for the proliferation of diverse narratives, each reflecting the biases and perspectives of its creators and transmitters.

The myth of Kublai Khan as a powerful, almost mystical figure, capable of controlling vast territories and influencing events across continents, also plays a significant role. This image, frequently present in popular culture and literature, elevates him to near-legendary status. This perception frequently overshadows the practical challenges he faced in governing such a diverse and geographically expansive empire, emphasizing the romantic ideal of imperial rule over the logistical and political difficulties of actually governing it. It creates a simplified vision of leadership that neglects the complex web of internal politics and external pressures he constantly navigated.

Furthermore, the interweaving of fact and fiction in many accounts has further complicated our understanding. Tales of his immense wealth, his exotic court, and his encounters with legendary figures have become inextricably linked with historical events, making it challenging to separate verifiable information from imaginative embellishments. This merging of reality and mythology contributes to the enduring fascination with Kublai Khan but also makes it increasingly difficult to establish a definitive and balanced assessment of his impact.

In conclusion, the myths surrounding Kublai Khan have significantly impacted our perception of his legacy. While these narratives sometimes distort historical accuracy, they reveal much about the cultural and societal values of the eras in which they were created and transmitted. Analyzing these myths, therefore, offers not just an understanding of Kublai Khan himself, but also a window into the evolving interpretations of power, empire, and cultural exchange across centuries.

20. Kublai Khan in Art and Literature

The Portrayal of Kublai Khan in Various Forms of Art and Literature Throughout History

Kublai Khan,

a figure of immense historical significance, has captivated the imagination of artists and writers for centuries. His portrayal across diverse mediums reflects not only the evolution of historical understanding but also the cultural and political contexts in which these interpretations were created. From early chronicles to modern novels and films, Kublai Khan's image has undergone a fascinating metamorphosis, shifting from a powerful, albeit sometimes brutal, conqueror to a complex and multifaceted leader.

Early historical accounts, often penned by those within or closely connected to his court, presented Kublai Khan as a <u>magnificent</u> and <u>wise emperor</u>. Marco Polo's *Travels*, while undeniably coloured by the Venetian's own experiences and biases, played a pivotal role in shaping the Western perception of Kublai Khan. Polo's depiction, though arguably romanticized, showcased a sophisticated and cosmopolitan court, filled with opulence and intrigue, highlighting Kublai Khan's grand scale of operations and the diversity of his empire. This early portrait established the foundation for many subsequent interpretations.

However, as historical understanding evolved, so too did the portrayal of Kublai Khan. Later Chinese chronicles, written from the perspective of the conquered, often presented a more nuanced and sometimes critical view. These accounts acknowledged his achievements in unifying China and fostering economic growth but also highlighted the oppression and resistance experienced by some segments of the population under his rule. This contrast provided a more complete, albeit multifaceted, picture, avoiding the simplistic glorification or demonization seen in earlier accounts.

The romantic and adventurous spirit of the 19th and early 20th centuries saw Kublai Khan portrayed in a myriad of novels and plays, often focusing on his relationship with Marco Polo and the exotic allure of his court. These works, while sometimes lacking historical accuracy, captured the public's imagination, firmly establishing Kublai Khan as a figure of romance and adventure in popular culture. This romanticisation, however, often overshadowed the complexities of his political maneuvering and the realities of his reign.

More recent portrayals in literature and film attempt to address this historical imbalance. There is a marked tendency towards a more critical and balanced assessment, acknowledging both his achievements and his flaws. Modern historians and writers often delve into the social and cultural impacts of his rule, exploring the intricacies of Mongol-Chinese relations and the legacy of his Yuan Dynasty. This newer scholarship shapes artistic interpretations, leading to portrayals that emphasize the internal conflicts, the cultural syncretism, and the complexities of governing such a vast and diverse empire.

In the visual arts, Kublai Khan's image has evolved alongside these literary representations. Early depictions often showcase him in regal attire, emphasizing his imperial power and majesty. However, more contemporary art incorporates a wider range of interpretations, reflecting the nuances of his character and the multifaceted nature of his reign. Some works depict him as a shrewd strategist, while others highlight his patronage of the arts and his interest in cultural exchange. The varied artistic expressions—from paintings and sculptures to graphic novels and video games—showcase a diverse tapestry of perspectives on this historical figure.

In conclusion, the portrayal of Kublai Khan in art and literature reflects a continuous dialogue between historical fact and artistic interpretation. While earlier representations were frequently idealized or demonized, more recent portrayals strive for a more nuanced and balanced understanding. From the romanticized accounts of Marco Polo to the critical analyses of modern historians, the evolution of Kublai Khan's image mirrors the ever-evolving nature of historical understanding itself. His story continues to fascinate and inspire, offering a rich canvas for artistic expression and scholarly debate.

Examining the artistic interpretations of his life, reign, and personality.

Kublai Khan's image has been shaped and reshaped across centuries, reflecting the evolving perceptions of his rule and the cultural contexts in which he was depicted. From grandiose imperial portraits to subtle details in everyday objects, the artistic record offers a fascinating lens through which to explore the complexities of his legacy.

Early depictions, often found in Yuan Dynasty official artwork, portray Kublai Khan as a powerful and majestic figure. These images emphasize his imperial authority, often showing him in regal attire, surrounded by symbols of power and wealth. Think of the meticulously crafted silk banners and imperial portraits designed to project an image of absolute sovereignty. The careful choice of colors, the grandeur of his robes, and the detail of his facial features – all were intended to communicate his divine right to rule and the splendor of his court. These early artistic renderings often incorporated Buddhist and Taoist influences, reflecting the religious syncretism that characterized his reign.

As centuries passed, the artistic interpretations shifted, influenced by changing historical narratives and artistic trends. The Ming Dynasty, for instance, often presented a more nuanced portrayal, acknowledging both his achievements and his failures. Artists of this period might emphasize aspects of his personality or specific events in his reign, sometimes to highlight the eventual decline of the Yuan dynasty. Note the subtle shifts in facial expression seen in these later portrayals, suggesting a greater depth of character and a more critical perspective on his reign.

The arrival of Western artists and travelers, particularly following Marco Polo's accounts, introduced new styles and perspectives. These artists, often working from secondhand descriptions and accounts, frequently presented a romanticized vision of Kublai Khan, influenced by the exotic allure of the East. The European-style portraits emerging during this period often emphasized his imperial grandeur and sophistication, frequently drawing upon stereotypical depictions of Mongol rulers.

Beyond official portraits and large-scale paintings, Kublai Khan's image permeates a wide variety of artistic forms. Consider the ceramic artifacts, jade carvings, and metalwork produced during the Yuan Dynasty, many incorporating symbolic motifs and designs associated with his reign. Even seemingly mundane objects, such as coins and everyday utensils, often bear subtle references to Kublai Khan or his dynasty, underscoring his ubiquitous influence on the daily lives of his subjects.

Moreover, the impact of Kublai Khan extends to the realm of literature. Many plays, poems, and novels, both during his reign and subsequently, feature Kublai Khan as a central figure. These literary representations often elaborate on various aspects of his character, building upon the existing artistic images and introducing new interpretations based on historical events and creative imagination. These literary works highlight different facets of his personality, from his military acumen and political shrewdness to his cultural sensitivity and personal vulnerabilities.

In conclusion, the artistic interpretations of Kublai Khan's life, reign, and personality constitute a complex and evolving tapestry, shaped by diverse cultural forces and perspectives across time. From the majestic imperial portraits to the subtle allusions in everyday objects and the vivid characterizations in literature, these artistic expressions provide a rich and nuanced understanding of this pivotal historical figure, reminding us that the 'truth' about any historical figure is often multifaceted and dependent on the lens through which it is viewed.

Analyzing how artistic representations have contributed to the historical understanding of Kublai Khan.

The multifaceted legacy of Kublai Khan, a figure pivotal in bridging East and West, has been profoundly shaped and interpreted through various artistic representations throughout history. These artistic depictions, ranging from grand imperial portraits to subtle details in literary works and everyday artifacts, offer valuable, albeit sometimes biased, insights into his reign, personality, and lasting impact. Analyzing these representations allows us to move beyond simple biographical accounts and grapple with the complexities of his historical significance.

Early portrayals of Kublai Khan, often commissioned by the Yuan court itself, tended to emphasize his imperial power and authority. These official artistic renderings, usually grand in scale and rich in symbolic detail, depicted him in majestic robes, surrounded by court officials and symbols of his power, such as the imperial seal or the banners of his armies. The intention was clearly to project an image of absolute sovereignty and divinely ordained rule, a common strategy in imperial iconography. These works, though imbued with propagandistic elements, offer valuable insights into the Yuan court's self-perception and the desired image it projected to both its subjects and the outside world. They reveal the stylistic preferences and artistic conventions prevalent during his era, offering a glimpse into the tastes and sensibilities of the Yuan court and its cultural aspirations.

In contrast, later depictions, particularly those emerging after the Yuan Dynasty's decline, often reflect shifting perspectives and interpretations of his reign. For instance, Ming Dynasty artistic representations may have downplayed or even subtly criticized aspects of Mongol rule, reflecting a nationalist sentiment seeking to emphasize the restoration of Han Chinese dominance. The manner in which Kublai Khan's physical features were portrayed – emphasizing his Mongol heritage or downplaying it – provides a subtle yet important clue to the prevailing political climate and the intentions of the artist.

The writings of Marco Polo, while not strictly artistic in the traditional sense, significantly influenced artistic perceptions of Kublai Khan in the West. Polo's vivid descriptions of the grandeur of Khanbaliq and the richness of the Yuan court inspired countless illustrations and artistic interpretations in European art, often romanticizing or exoticizing the Mongol emperor and his court. These depictions, though based on secondhand accounts and filtered through European cultural biases, fueled the European imagination about the East and contributed to the enduring myths and legends surrounding Kublai Khan, shaping perceptions far beyond the historical accuracy of Polo's account.

The development of printing technology in both East and West also played a crucial role. Woodblock prints in China and later, engravings in Europe, allowed for the wider dissemination of images of Kublai Khan, further shaping his visual legacy. These readily reproducible images democratized access to his image, albeit often in simplified or stylized forms, perpetuating certain aspects of his persona and contributing to popular understanding, which often diverged from more nuanced scholarly accounts.

Furthermore, contemporary art and literature continue to engage with Kublai Khan's image. Modern artists have reinterpreted his life and reign, drawing on historical accounts but also incorporating modern sensibilities and perspectives. These contemporary works often engage with themes of cultural exchange, empire building, and the complex relationship between power and identity, reflecting our current historical and cultural understanding.

In conclusion, the artistic representations of Kublai Khan are not simply passive reflections of historical reality, but rather active agents in shaping our understanding of him. Analyzing these representations, recognizing both their potential biases and their intrinsic value, provides a rich and multifaceted understanding of this pivotal historical figure, revealing not only his historical impact but also the evolving ways in which cultures remember and reinterpret their past.

21. Comparative Studies: Kublai Khan and other Great Rulers

Comparing and contrasting Kublai Khan's reign with those of other renowned historical figures.

*Kublai Khan, the fifth Khagan of the Mongol Empire and founder of the Yuan dynasty, stands as a fascinating figure for comparative historical analysis. His reign, marked by both **breathtaking expansion and significant cultural exchange**, invites comparison with other rulers who navigated similar challenges of empire building, multi-ethnic governance, and lasting legacies.*

A compelling comparison emerges when juxtaposing Kublai Khan with **Augustus Caesar**. Both inherited power within complex political landscapes, consolidating authority through shrewd diplomacy and military prowess. Augustus, emerging from the chaos of the Roman Republic, established the Pax Romana, a period of relative peace and prosperity. Similarly, Kublai Khan, following the conquests of Genghis Khan, brought a degree of stability to a vast, multi-cultural empire, fostering trade along the Silk Road and promoting economic growth. However, their approaches differed. Augustus focused on *internal consolidation* and the creation of a strong centralized state, while Kublai Khan's efforts focused on *managing a diverse* *empire* through a more decentralized system, often accommodating existing local structures and administrative practices.

Comparing Kublai Khan to Ashoka the Great reveals a contrasting approach to empire management. Ashoka, after a bloody conquest of India, embraced Buddhism and implemented policies of non-violence and social welfare. While Kublai Khan practiced **religious tolerance**, his empire was built on military conquest and maintained through considerable force. Both rulers, however, sought to leave a positive societal impact, with Ashoka focusing on *moral transformation* and Kublai Khan on *economic prosperity and cultural exchange*. Ashoka's edicts emphasized dharma and social justice, while Kublai Khan's policies fostered trade and infrastructure development, indicating their distinct approaches to achieving societal good.

A further comparison with Akbar the Great of the Mughal Empire highlights the complexities of multi-cultural rule. Both rulers presided over vast empires with diverse populations and religions. Akbar, known for his **religious tolerance and administrative reforms**, implemented policies that integrated Hindus and Muslims, while Kublai Khan adopted a similar approach, albeit with a more pragmatic balance of power between the Mongol elite and the Chinese bureaucracy. While both rulers attempted to bridge cultural divides through *religious tolerance and administrative strategies*, the specific mechanisms and long-term consequences differed greatly depending on the existing social structures and cultural landscapes of their empires.

The contrasting reigns of Kublai Khan and Alexander the Great emphasize the varying impact of conquest.

Alexander's short but incredibly impactful reign was characterized by rapid military expansion across Persia, India, and Egypt. He left behind a legacy of cultural fusion, though his empire fragmented soon after his death. Kublai Khan's reign, while also spanning extensive territories, saw a longer period of relative stability and the establishment of a lasting dynasty. Though the Yuan dynasty eventually fell, its influence on China and East Asia remains significant. The difference in their empires' longevities stemmed partly from different approaches to governance and integration of conquered territories, with Kublai Khan showing a greater commitment to institutionalizing his rule compared to Alexander's relatively short tenure.

In conclusion, comparing Kublai Khan's reign to those of Augustus, Ashoka, Akbar, and Alexander reveals both similarities and stark contrasts. While all these rulers faced the challenges of empire-building and managing diverse populations, their approaches to governance, cultural interaction, and long-term legacies varied significantly. Kublai Khan's emphasis on **cultural exchange and economic development** within a vast, multi-ethnic context set his reign apart, highlighting the unique dynamics of the Mongol Empire's influence on global history.

Analyzing commonalities and differences in their leadership styles, accomplishments, and legacies.

A Comparative Study of Kublai Khan and Other Great Rulers

To fully grasp the significance of Kublai Khan's reign, a comparative analysis with other prominent historical figures is crucial. This exploration will delve into the commonalities and disparities in their leadership styles, accomplishments, and enduring legacies, ultimately enriching our understanding of Kublai Khan's unique place in history.

One compelling comparison is with **Alexander the Great**. Both rulers exhibited exceptional military prowess, conquering vast territories and establishing expansive empires. Alexander, through his unparalleled tactical brilliance and relentless ambition, forged a massive empire spanning from Greece to India in a relatively short timeframe. Similarly, Kublai Khan, inheriting and expanding the Mongol Empire, orchestrated impressive military campaigns, culminating in the establishment of the Yuan Dynasty, a powerful and influential realm. However, their approaches to governance differed significantly. Alexander's empire, while initially successful, fragmented rapidly after his death due to a lack of centralized administration and a clear succession plan. Kublai Khan, on the other hand, implemented sophisticated administrative reforms, establishing a complex bureaucratic structure, and fostering a degree of cultural integration that promoted stability, at least for a time, within his diverse empire. This speaks volumes about the long-term vision that underpinned Kublai Khan's strategies.

Another interesting parallel can be drawn with **Emperor Augustus of Rome**. Both leaders inherited power within pre-existing empires but consolidated and transformed them through their own considerable abilities. Augustus, following the tumultuous years of the Roman Republic, ushered in a period of relative peace and prosperity, the Pax Romana. He skillfully navigated political complexities, reforming the Roman state and establishing an enduring imperial system. Kublai Khan faced similar challenges, inheriting a vast, albeit fractured, empire and establishing a new dynasty. Like Augustus, Kublai Khan implemented crucial administrative reforms and economic policies that fostered stability and economic growth. While Augustus focused on solidifying Roman power within the Mediterranean, Kublai Khan's ambitions extended beyond the immediate sphere of influence, reaching out to far-flung nations through ambitious trade initiatives along the Silk Road.

Conversely, significant differences exist. Unlike Augustus' careful, gradual consolidation of power, Kublai Khan's ascent was marked by rapid military conquests and the integration of diverse cultures. While both were skilled diplomats, Kublai Khan's interactions with foreign powers were arguably more complex, characterized by both diplomacy and military expansionism. The legacies, while impressive, are also distinct. Augustus's legacy is fundamentally Roman, centered on the consolidation of power and the Pax Romana. Kublai Khan's legacy, however, is more multifaceted, reflecting his unique position as the ruler of a vast empire that bridged East and West, leaving behind a complex legacy of cultural exchange and the fusion of disparate traditions, notably Mongol and Chinese cultures.

A comparison with **Ashoka the Great of India** highlights additional contrasts. Ashoka's empire, while geographically smaller, was consolidated through powerful military campaigns, followed by a profound shift in his governing philosophy, characterized by a strong emphasis on non-violence and Buddhist principles. While Kublai Khan was known for his religious tolerance and patronage of various faiths, his rule wasn't fundamentally defined by a similar paradigm shift. His empire's growth was less tied to religious ideology and more driven by strategic ambitions. This difference reflects contrasting approaches to leadership and governance, with Ashoka emphasizing dharma and moral leadership and Kublai Khan prioritizing political stability and economic prosperity alongside a practical approach to cultural adaptation.

In conclusion, while Kublai Khan shares some similarities with other great rulers in terms of military prowess, administrative skills, and the establishment of powerful empires, the nuances of his leadership style, accomplishments, and legacy remain unique. His ability to effectively manage a vast and diverse empire, fostering significant cultural exchange and economic growth, sets him apart. By studying these comparisons, we gain a richer understanding of his accomplishments and the enduring impact of his reign, solidifying his position as a truly exceptional and influential figure in world history. His life and reign serve as a complex case study that continues to inspire debate and further research on leadership, empire building, and the dynamics of cultural interaction.

Gaining a Deeper Understanding of Kublai Khan's Unique Place in History.

Kublai Khan's legacy transcends the simple categorization of "great ruler." To truly understand his unique place in history requires moving beyond the conventional narratives of conquest and empire-building, delving into the complexities of his reign and its lasting impact on a global scale.

Unlike many conquerors driven primarily by military ambition, Kublai Khan demonstrated a keen understanding of the **interconnectedness** of cultures and economies. His reign witnessed an unprecedented flourishing of the Silk Road, not merely as a conduit for trade, but as a vibrant artery of cultural exchange. This wasn't merely opportunistic exploitation; Kublai Khan actively **cultivated** this exchange, recognizing its potential to strengthen his empire and enrich its diverse populace.

His approach to governance was equally nuanced. While he inherited the formidable military might of the Mongol Empire, he also understood the **necessity of integration** rather than outright subjugation. His policies, while sometimes harsh, ultimately aimed at creating a unified and prosperous empire, incorporating elements of Chinese administration and legal systems while retaining core Mongol traditions. This synthesis, though often fraught with tension, represents a **unique experiment** in imperial governance, distinct from the purely assimilationist or exploitative approaches of other historical empires.

The **cultural synthesis** under Kublai Khan wasn't merely superficial. His court became a melting pot of different religions and belief systems—Buddhism, Taoism, Confucianism, Islam, and even Christianity—coexisting (albeit not always harmoniously) within the same framework. This relative religious tolerance, though not absolute, stands in stark contrast to many contemporaneous rulers who enforced strict religious conformity. His patronage of the arts and learning further fostered a vibrant cultural landscape, resulting in a uniquely blended Yuan dynasty aesthetic that reflected the diverse influences of his empire.

Kublai Khan's interaction with figures like Marco Polo adds another layer to his complexity. While the veracity of Polo's accounts remains debated, their influence on the Western perception of the East is undeniable. Polo's narrative, regardless of its accuracy, helped shape the European imagination of the Far East, contributing to the gradual expansion of global trade and intercultural understanding—a consequence, albeit indirect, of Kublai Khan's reign.

However, focusing solely on the positive aspects would be an incomplete picture. Kublai Khan's reign was also marked by military failures, such as the disastrous campaigns against Japan, and internal rebellions that challenged his authority. These setbacks highlight the inherent limitations of even the most powerful empires, demonstrating that his achievements were not effortless and his success was always contingent on a complex interplay of factors.

Ultimately, Kublai Khan's unique place in history stems from the **paradoxical nature** of his legacy. He was a conqueror who sought integration, a military leader who fostered cultural exchange, an absolute ruler who demonstrated a degree of tolerance. His reign, a complex tapestry of success and failure, provides invaluable insights into the challenges and opportunities of empire building, cultural interaction, and the enduring complexities of leadership on a global scale. Understanding his unique place demands acknowledging both the grandeur of his achievements and the limitations of his power, revealing a far more nuanced and compelling historical figure than simplistic narratives allow.

The study of Kublai Khan is not just a study of a single ruler; it is a window into the dynamics of a pivotal era in world history—an era defined by the intersection of East and West, the rise and fall of empires, and the enduring legacy of cultural exchange. His story transcends the boundaries of time and geography, continuing to resonate with scholars and the general public alike.

His story serves as a reminder that *history is rarely black and white*. It is a tapestry woven with threads of ambition, diplomacy, brutality, and tolerance, creating a portrait of a leader whose actions continue to shape our understanding of global history.

22. Kublai Khan's Legacy for Future Generations

The Long-Term Impact of Kublai Khan's Reign on the World

Kublai Khan's reign, though ultimately finite, cast a long shadow across the tapestry of world history. His impact resonates even today, a testament to the enduring consequences of his leadership and the transformative era he shaped.

One of the most significant and lasting impacts of Kublai Khan's reign was the unification and expansion of the Mongol Empire. He oversaw a period of relative stability and prosperity within the vast empire, facilitating unprecedented levels of trade and cultural exchange. This interconnectedness, fostered by the Pax Mongolica, facilitated the movement of goods, ideas, and technologies across Eurasia, leaving an indelible mark on the global economic landscape. The Silk Road flourished under his rule, connecting East and West in ways never before seen, stimulating economic growth and facilitating cultural diffusion on an unprecedented scale. The resultant economic integration propelled technological advancements and fostered a vibrant exchange of goods, ideas, and religious beliefs across continents.

Beyond the economic impact, Kublai Khan's reign significantly influenced the cultural landscape of Eurasia. His embrace of religious tolerance led to a unique blending of cultures within the Yuan Dynasty. Buddhism, Taoism, Confucianism, Islam, and Christianity coexisted, creating a melting pot of religious and philosophical thought. This religious diversity, though not always without its tensions, fostered intellectual exchange and creative innovation. His patronage of the arts and sciences further enriched this cultural dynamism. The architectural marvels of Khanbaliq (present-day Beijing), a testament to the fusion of Mongol and Chinese architectural styles, stand as a lasting symbol of this cultural synthesis. This period saw a blossoming of art, literature, and scholarship, shaped by the interplay of various cultural traditions. The legacy of this cultural cross-pollination continues to influence artistic expression and intellectual discourse today.

However, the long-term effects of Kublai Khan's rule were not solely positive. The extensive military campaigns, while expanding the empire's reach, also placed considerable strain on its resources and contributed to internal instability. The failed invasions of Japan and Vietnam highlighted the limitations of Mongol military might, underscoring the difficulties inherent in governing such a vast and diverse empire. The subsequent decline of the Yuan Dynasty serves as a reminder that even the most powerful empires are subject to internal strife and external pressures. The internal challenges of managing a multi-ethnic and multi-religious empire, and the struggles to balance the needs of different populations, had a lasting impact on the political landscape of the region for centuries to come.

Furthermore, Kublai Khan's legacy is intertwined with the long-term impact of the Mongol Empire on the global order. The Mongol conquests and subsequent administrative structures reshaped political boundaries, trade routes, and power dynamics across a vast

201

geographical expanse. The Pax Mongolica, while contributing to increased trade and connectivity, also resulted in significant population displacement and the disruption of traditional societies. The long-term effects of this period of intense expansion continue to be debated and analyzed by historians, encompassing everything from demographic shifts to the spread of diseases.

In conclusion, the long-term impact of Kublai Khan's reign extends far beyond the confines of his lifetime and the geographical extent of the Yuan Dynasty. His reign represents a pivotal moment in world history, a period marked by unprecedented trade and cultural exchange, yet also challenged by the inherent difficulties of managing a vast and diverse empire. His legacy is a complex tapestry woven from threads of prosperity and conflict, cultural fusion and political upheaval. It serves as a compelling case study in the complexities of imperial power, the enduring influence of cultural exchange, and the lasting impact of a single ruler on the global stage. His reign continues to shape how we understand global history, trade, cultural interaction, and the rise and fall of empires.

His lasting contributions to governance, economics, and cultural exchange.

Kublai Khan's reign, though marked by both triumphs and tribulations, left an indelible mark on the governance, economy, and cultural landscape of the vast Yuan Empire, impacting the course of history in profound and lasting ways.

In the realm of <u>governance</u>, Kublai Khan implemented significant administrative reforms. He established a centralized bureaucratic system, drawing inspiration from both Mongol traditions and the sophisticated Chinese model. This involved a complex interplay of Mongol officials and Chinese scholars, a strategy designed to integrate the strengths of both cultures and manage the vast, diverse empire effectively. While facing challenges in reconciling disparate legal systems and administrative practices, his efforts laid the foundation for a more unified governance structure. His adoption of a modified version of the Chinese examination system, albeit with limitations, demonstrated an attempt to integrate Chinese talent within the administrative framework, a significant step toward political integration. The establishment of a new capital, Khanbaliq (modern-day Beijing), symbolized this fusion of cultures, showcasing a blend of Mongol and Chinese architectural styles and city planning. This strategic decision reflected his commitment to building a powerful and stable empire based on a synthesis of traditions.

His contributions to the **economy** were equally transformative. Kublai Khan, recognizing the importance of trade and commerce, actively promoted the growth of the Silk Road. He fostered a climate conducive to international trade, enacting policies that encouraged merchants from across Eurasia to traverse his vast domains. This led to a period of unprecedented economic prosperity, with the Yuan Dynasty becoming a major player in global trade. The influx of foreign goods and ideas fueled economic growth, enriched the cultural landscape, and connected the East and West in ways previously unseen. His government invested heavily in infrastructure projects, such as the construction and repair of canals and roads, facilitating trade and improving the flow of goods across the empire. These ambitious undertakings not only stimulated the economy but also fostered a sense of unity and connection within the diverse populations under his rule. This economic flourishing, however, was not without its complexities, with challenges arising from managing a vast economic system and dealing with the intricacies of international commerce. The impact of these economic policies remained significant long after his death.

Perhaps most strikingly, Kublai Khan championed *cultural exchange* and religious tolerance. His court became a melting pot of cultures, attracting scholars, artists, and artisans from across Eurasia. He actively patronized the arts and encouraged the synthesis of Mongol, Chinese, and foreign artistic traditions. This fostered a dynamic period of creativity and cultural innovation, resulting in unique artistic expressions that blended diverse influences. His policy of religious tolerance allowed for the peaceful coexistence of Buddhism, Taoism, Confucianism, Islam, and Christianity, a testament to his relatively open-minded approach to faith and belief. This fostering of diverse cultural and religious traditions did not necessarily mean perfect harmony, but it contributed to a period of relative peace and cultural innovation, showcasing the potential benefits of cross-cultural dialogue. Marco Polo's famous accounts vividly illustrate the cosmopolitan nature of Kublai Khan's court, emphasizing its role as a bridge between East and West, a space where cultures could interact and exchange ideas.

In conclusion, Kublai Khan's lasting contributions to governance, economics, and cultural exchange shaped the Yuan Dynasty and left a profound impact on the course of history. His administrative reforms, economic policies, and promotion of cultural exchange demonstrate a complex and multifaceted legacy, a blend of success and failure that continues to fascinate and challenge historians today. His reign stands as a significant chapter in the history of both China and the world, showcasing the possibilities and challenges of empire-building in a multicultural environment.

His Importance as a Pivotal Figure in History

Kublai Khan's enduring significance transcends the confines of his era, resonating deeply within the tapestry of global history. His impact is multifaceted, leaving an indelible mark on political structures, economic systems, and cultural landscapes across Eurasia.

As the founder of the Yuan Dynasty, Kublai Khan fundamentally reshaped the political and administrative framework of China. His reign witnessed the integration of Mongol and Chinese cultures, a complex process marked by both conflict and collaboration. This fusion, while often fraught with tension, ultimately yielded a unique cultural synthesis that left its imprint on Chinese art, literature, and society for centuries. The legacy of the Yuan Dynasty's administrative systems and its impact on subsequent Chinese dynasties continues to be a subject of rigorous historical investigation, highlighting its enduring relevance.

Kublai Khan's influence extended far beyond the borders of his empire. His reign coincided with a period of unprecedented expansion and prosperity along the Silk Road. His policies fostered an environment of increased trade and cultural exchange between East and West, connecting distant civilizations and facilitating the movement of goods, ideas, and people across vast distances. The economic impact of this increased connectivity profoundly altered global trade patterns and laid the foundation for future economic growth in Eurasia. Even today, scholars continue to examine the economic and societal implications of the flourishing trade networks established under his rule.

Furthermore, Kublai Khan's reign represents a significant chapter in the history of global exploration. His court welcomed travelers and emissaries from distant lands, including the famed Marco Polo, whose accounts provided Europeans with their first detailed glimpse into the wonders of the East. These interactions broadened intercultural understanding, albeit sometimes through a lens of cultural bias, shaping European perceptions of the Orient for centuries. The exchange of knowledge and technology fueled by this interaction played a crucial role in fostering global interconnectedness.

However, Kublai Khan's legacy is not without its complexities. His military campaigns, while expanding the empire's reach, also resulted in significant human costs. His attempts to conquer Japan, for instance, ended in disastrous defeat. This underscores the inherent limitations of imperial power and the unpredictable nature of military ventures, even for a leader as capable and resourceful as Kublai Khan. His failures, like his successes, offer valuable insights into the dynamics of imperial expansion and the challenges of maintaining control over a vast, diverse empire. The study of his reign provides a case study in the complex interplay of ambition, strategy, and unforeseen consequences that shape the course of history.

In conclusion, Kublai Khan's importance as a pivotal historical figure stems from his profound impact on political systems, economic structures, and cultural exchange across Eurasia. His reign represents a critical juncture in the history of global interconnection, leaving a lasting legacy that continues to fascinate and inspire debate among historians and scholars. The complexity and multifaceted nature of his legacy serve as a powerful reminder of the enduring influence of individuals who shaped the course of history, even with their successes and failures intertwined.

—A Comprehensive Analysis of Kublai Khan's Enduring Impact

23. Conclusion: Bridging the Past and Present

Kublai Khan's life and reign, a tapestry woven with threads of conquest, diplomacy, and cultural exchange, offers a compelling lens through which to examine the complexities of empire-building and cross-cultural interaction.

From his humble beginnings as a grandson of Genghis Khan to his ascension as the founder of the Yuan Dynasty, Kublai's journey was marked by both strategic brilliance and inherent contradictions. His military prowess, evident in his subjugation of the Southern Song Dynasty, stands in stark contrast to his surprising embrace of Chinese culture and his promotion of religious tolerance. This paradoxical nature is a recurring theme throughout his life, challenging simplistic narratives and demanding a nuanced understanding.

The **establishment of Khanbaliq**, his magnificent capital, serves as a potent symbol of this fusion of cultures. The city's architecture, a blend of Mongol pragmatism and Chinese aesthetic sophistication, reflects the intricate interplay of power and adaptation that characterized his rule. The flourishing of trade along the **Silk Road** under his reign underscores his understanding of the economic advantages of interconnectedness and the symbiotic relationship between commerce and cultural exchange. His patronage of arts and his tolerant approach towards various religions – Buddhism, Taoism, Confucianism, Islam, and Christianity – fostered a period of unprecedented cultural synthesis, solidifying the Yuan Dynasty's unique identity.

However, the narrative of Kublai Khan is not one of unmitigated success. His ambitious military campaigns in Southeast Asia and Japan, while showcasing his aggressive expansionist tendencies, ultimately ended in failure, highlighting the limits of even the most formidable empire. Internal strife, rebellions, and the inherent challenges of governing a vast and diverse realm cast a shadow over his achievements. The integration of Mongol and Chinese cultures, while fostering periods of prosperity and innovation, also faced significant obstacles and resulted in persistent social and political tensions.

Marco Polo's account, while arguably embellished, offers a valuable, albeit skewed, glimpse into the grandeur and complexity of Kublai's court. The Venetian's narrative, though open to debate in terms of accuracy, cemented the Yuan Dynasty's place in the Western imagination and forever linked the name of Kublai Khan with the legendary Silk Road, underscoring the lasting impact of his reign on global perceptions.

The *legacy of Kublai Khan* remains a subject of ongoing scholarly debate. Historians continue to grapple with the complexities of his character and reign, interpreting his actions through diverse lenses and considering the varied perspectives of those who lived under his rule. Examining the differing interpretations of his life and times, from the glowing accounts of his supporters to the critical assessments of his adversaries, is crucial for a comprehensive understanding of this pivotal figure.

Ultimately, the study of Kublai Khan transcends a simple biography. His story provides a rich case study in the dynamics of empire building, the challenges of cross-cultural integration, and the enduring impact of leadership on the course of history. By examining his successes and failures, his innovations and shortcomings, we gain valuable insights not only into the intricacies of the Yuan Dynasty but also into the universal themes of power, ambition, cultural exchange, and the enduring human quest for connection across geographical and cultural boundaries. Kublai Khan's life, therefore, serves as a bridge connecting the distant past to our present, offering valuable lessons about the complexities of governance, the enduring power of cultural synthesis, and the enduring impact of individual leaders on the shaping of global history. His story continues to resonate, a reminder of the enduring legacy of empire and the persistent search for harmony amidst diversity.

– A Reflection on the Enduring Impact of Kublai Khan

Printed in Great Britain
by Amazon

61870051R00122